CALIFORNIA'S NEXT CENTURY 2.0

Title: California's Next Century 2.0: Economic Renaissance©

Author(s): Marcus Ruiz Evans

Publisher: Mikazuki Publishing House

ISBN-13: 978-1-937981-81-5 (Print)

I0022410

Author: Marcus Ruiz Evans

With editing by John English, and Jennifer Herschbach To: Marshall McLuhan, Eric Hoffer, Jared Diamond, Mancur Olson, Leopold Kohr, John Lott Jr., John Howard Griffin, William Herschel, Phillip Bobbitt, and Alex Salmond.

CALIFORNIA'S NEXT CENTURY 2.0

TABLE OF CONTENTS:

CALIFORNIA'S NEXT CENTURY 2.0

Appendixes

CALIFORNIA'S NEXT CENTURY 2.0

"Make everything as simple as possible, but not simpler." —Albert Einstein

"Few modern ideologies are as whimsically all-encompassing, as romantically obscure, as intellectually sloppy, and as likely to start a third world war as the theory of 'geopolitics.'" —Charles Clover, "Dreams of the Eurasian Heartland: The Reemergence of Geopolitics" *Foreign Affairs*, March/April 1999

"...As the paradigmatic means of choosing among research projects and, more recently, programmatic awards and grants for new research centers and national science and engineering facilities, sometimes has the effect of suppressing consideration of public values." —Dan Sarewitzand, and Barry Bozeman , *Public Failures in US Science Policy*, (Washington, D.C.: Center for Science Policy and Outcomes, 2002): 12

"Thus it is that we can say that the capitalist world-economy has now entered its terminal crisis, a crisis that may last up to fifty years. The real question before us is what will happen during this crisis, this transition from the present world-system to some other king of historical system or systems." —

CALIFORNIA'S NEXT CENTURY 2.0

Immanuel Wallerstein "Globalization or the age of transition?: A long-term view of the trajectory of the world-system," *International Sociology*, Volume: 15, Issue: 2, (2000) : 249-265

"The discrepancy in power, as between California and the other western states, has strikingly augmented this tendency on the part of the people to think of California as a province apart, a sovereign in its own right, a self-contained empire. The very scale by which happenings, events, and developments are measured in the freakish environment of California makes it extremely difficult for Californians to relate their problems to those of the other western states. The environment, in other words, tends to distort the perspective of those who dwell within the state." —Carey McWilliams, *California: The Great Exception* (UC Press, 1940), 364.

CALIFORNIA'S NEXT CENTURY 2.0

FOREWORD:

It has only been a few months since I have been taking the message of what California's next Century could be to the people, and I wanted to document the response so far for this new updated version of the book. I have given the almost identical speech at 12 California cities so far, available on YouTube, under Marcus Ruiz Evans. I talked about how people could have less taxes and bureaucracy and more control over the decisions of almost all policies that affect their lives, and could have an economy that would be the center of all of the energy of the world, and would therefore make California recession proof – forever.

I spoke in, SD, Berkeley, SF, West Hollywood twice, Modesto, Santa Rosa, Glendora, San Jose, Moraga, South SF, and Fresno, and Clovis. Cities that are in the far north, the liberal Bay Area, the conservative Central Valley, and the media center of Southern California, and the more conservative SD area. The response at each area, has been almost exactly the same. On average, for every 2 people who are incensed by the discussion of becoming something other than an average state in America, there are 10 people who are fascinated by the concept. Not that these people agree, but that they the proposal of the book definately worth exploring. Of these 10, the majority, 6+ people on average, were interested in the idea before I even explained any of the concepts behind it. They matched the original research before I wrote this book – that there is already an inherent interest in Californians about this concept.

CALIFORNIA'S NEXT CENTURY 2.0

Here are the major observations I have made so far, reaching out to the people of California, about California's next century:

A) As I expected, the people in the North, South, and Center of California, think alike, ask almost exactly the same questions, have almost exactly the same concerns, even though each region of California is convinced they are nothing like the other regions. Californians in each region were equally concerned by one particular question below – how can California achieve this?

B) People were curious as to what, exactly, this new California would look like – being the global center for the world's cultures and international business & having the ability to decide completely on their own, 98% of the policy issues that were primarily decided

historically by the Federal government?

The short answer is that the answer can only

come from a discussion of 40 million people.

This book is only to start the discussion, not to

fill it in, not to complete, not to argue for an

answer, but to light the imaginations of all

Californians, old enough to read and think about

the future, about what they could become. There

are a million details that would have to

determined to work out how California could be

a global center for the needs of the next century,

and how it would run itself if more like a nation-

state. I have been asked how would this affect

the political parties? Does the governor support

it? Do the Senators support it? How would it

affect Unions? What about third parties? I don't

know, is the unsatisfactory answer. The plan in the book is a proposal for what the future could be. I don't know what different political parties or current organizations opinions would be on it, because everything presented is hypothetical. But I can point out, what has already been talked about in the original version of the book, a message that is very popular at most cities, and that is how the plan in California's Next Century would affect business in California.

1. Taxes would be half of what they are now for all businesses. This would make the tax rate in California comparable to Singapore, Hong Kong, and Switzerland, the countries with the highest respect internationally for their tax rates.

2. Bureaucracy of every business would be cut in half, making operating in California 50% easier.

3. Students at all public schools would be taught business and finance, so they would be more intelligent in the future if they ever want to start a business, and to make the general public more understanding of the pressures of running a successful business.

4. Adult schools would offer business incubation classes – teaching adults already out of school, how to spot investment opportunities in their lives.

5. California's economy would effectively become Recession proof, meaning that investments in California would never go down due to an economic slump.

6. Because California's economy depended on being attractive as a nexus for global governments and business, the entire people and government of California, if they choose to move the state to enact this plan, would be more sensitive to business needs politically, and would be more concerned about producing people with the skills that businesses in California needed.

7. The government would also pursue options to make business easier in California, such as making all permit processes electronic and simplifying the application process. And buying and then offering for free, or developing to offer for free, software to navigate the government approval process, and management of a business in general, such as free ERP software provided by the taxpayers of the state, because they now, all understand the importance of a strong business environment for California's future plan into the next century.

C) The last observation was something that I didn't expect. That was which radical concepts from the book the public would be shocked by. Californian's were not shocked by these concepts from the book, although I thought they would be:

- Californians are unique in the world
- Californians are different from Americans
- Americans don't like Californians
- Americans stereotype Californians
- America uses and abuses California for money
- California could be its own country
- California is known around the world with a unique global identity
- California could be the world center for discussion amongst all cultures, because it

has that ability to house and reach out to all

cultures around the world better than any

other place on Earth

Most people did not ask for references or examples

for these points, although they are in the book.

People seemed to accept these points. However, in

cities in the North and the South, and in the Central

Valley, everyone was stuck on one question, - *"how*

will California not collapse under its own weight if

the Federal government is not there to take care of

it. I.e. Is California a marionette, who when the

strings are cut, will collapse under its own weight

when it is completely responsible for itself. This

plan sounds great, but California is able to exist

with all of its problems, because the Federal

government oversees us, and tells us how to run

everything properly. Without that, we would fall apart, almost instantly."

I did not expect this. People admit that California is unique in the World, and compared to America, and that America and the World both know this is a different and special place, full of wonder, and experimentation. With a long history of research, and pioneering new things because of an inherent California character. Yet, California should be careful of making this jump to a more independent place in the world, because the Federal government is the only thing keeping this state afloat. Although, everyone agrees that California routinely innovates new policies ahead of the Federal government or any other state, and these policies are often copied by the Federal government after California has worked them out, and used them for decades.

CALIFORNIA'S NEXT CENTURY 2.0

Insurance, health care, telecommunications,
internet, climate change, foreign trade, air quality,
Jewish holocaust recognition, are all examples.
People agree to this. And they agree that California
gives somewhere between $60-100 Billion away
ever year in extra money, paid for in Federal taxes,
that it never receives any services for. Money that
pays for other states. And they agree that the
Federal government has given California powers,
held for the Federal government typically, because
the Feds have acknowledged that they cannot run
certain area of California policy better than
California can on their own; Insurance, Climate
Change, Environmental Regulation, and Health
Care, are all examples.

Yet, even admitting to all of these dynamics about
the state of California, people still strongly question

if California could run its own government, effectively, on its own. I don't see how California hasn't already proven that – with giving a surplus of money into the national pot every year when it receives no money from others, with still being the world's 5-8th largest economy even with this money being drained out, with having the Federal government giving up powers on areas to California on the one hand, and on the other, with California not infrequently developing new areas of governance that the Federal government copies after California.

Because of this question being asked so universally by Californians, what I theorize, is that the only thing keeping this plan for what California could metamorphosis into, from happening, is doubt, by the people of California, on how great we are as Californians.

Someone asked me why Californians think this way. I theorized another answer, and I think it is correct, the more I look into it. All of the media companies in America are owned by a few companies based in the East Coast primarily. California news stations and news papers cover stories that are approved by the National office. Meaning that California news is ultimately approved and selected by people who have a national perspective and not a California one. The national perspective is that California costs the Union money, can never get its own act completely together, and is nothing but a financial drain and a source of constant new social problems for the rest of the states. Californians getting their news from national sources routinely hear this - not based on actual fact, national opinion - of California, and over time, through constantly hearing it, they begin to believe it.

The proof of my opinion is that when I site a few, positive statistics, of California, all found in the book, no one at any of the speeches across the state has ever heard of them. California developed trade policy, environmental policy, climate change policy, health care policy, insurance policy that the Federal government later copied. California has been rated by the Federal government as having the best money management of any state government, for multiple years. As having the most professional legislature, that works the most efficiently, and delivers bills that the public wants more than any other state government. This is not saying that

CALIFORNIA'S NEXT CENTURY 2.0

California does not have problems, but that
California deals with its issues better than any other
government could. I almost got into an argument
with a group of conservatives, asking in a truly
confused fashion *"where does this belief that the
Federal government could do anything any better
for us, than we can do for ourselves, especially
when you admit that California is different from
most of America, and that Americans don't think
like Californians. How can that be true, and yet, the
Federal government could still do a better job in
deciding what Californians need? Where does the
idea that the Federal government makes less
mistakes than the California government come
from? "*

A disturbing example of this dynamic of the people
of California, is an article published by California

Forward, a progressive think tank on California that is focused on providing hard factually positive news about the state and ways that it could move ahead. In an article "It takes a community" in August 17, 2009, by Robert M. Hertzberg and Thomas McKernan, both of whom work at California Forward, this depiction of California was given: "In the 2008 "Grading the States," an annual report published by the widely respected Pew Center on the States, California earned a C overall -- lower than 41 other states -- and a D-plus for its fiscal systems, tied with Rhode Island for dead last." What was left out, by an organization that is viewed as balanced, is that in that report, California was graded by the Federal government as excellent in; capital planning, project monitoring, inter-governmental coordination, performance auditing

and evaluation, and on-line services and
information. Meaning it was rated as excellent by
the Federal government in its ability to allocate
funds and ensure they were spent correctly
according to the wishes of the lay public. You
would never get the impression that California was
rated as anything other than a basket-case by
reading this report by a respected California think
tank. And yet, that is not what the actual report by
the Federal government said. The report pointed
out, but the article did not, that the main reason
California was graded so low by the Federal
government was because it laid off a massive
amount of government workers, and so had slowed
down its ability to operate effectively, in
comparison to other states that did not do massive
layoffs. California conducted the most layoffs of

any state because it was the hardest hit state in the 2008 Recession in all of America. Why was the positive news left out of this report? Why was the poor grade not explained? Why does a well researched, balanced, academic group, produce an article that only talks about how California is rated the worst in all of America?

The only answer that I can think of is that there is a MYTH, that California is a screw up state, and there are a people who only know the myth, and have never heard any of the facts.

This is a giant problem, if my analysis is correct, but it is also a giant opportunity. For if the only thing that is keeping Californians from opening up their hearts and minds to this plan fully, is a myth that California can't be anything but a screw up state on its own, then the moment, that the actual facts are brought into the light of day, of the mass of Californians, there will be no real barriers to 40 million people having the discussion about California's future in the next century, as presented in this book.

I.

The original title of this book was going to be either *How America Can Retain Its Global Lead of the Last Century—for the Next Century* or *A Realistic Plan for an Independent California* or *California's Independence, America's Salvation* and that should explain the dynamic of this book. The phrase California's Next Century (CNC), appears only in the second half of this book, after all of the discussion about the benefits of a change for America have been presented. This book is as much about saving and making a prosperous America as it is about California pursuing its own destiny. That is the key concept that this report most needs the reader to understand—that believing in ourselves as Californians is "The" path to protecting America's next century of existence.

The intent of the book is two-fold: for Americans to look at this strategy and discuss if they could be okay with this new future, and for the federal government to examine the details of enacting the ideas presented. In parallel with this goal is the intention that this book will not end but only start a controversy amongst average Californians. Do they think the future presented in this book is possible for those living in California? Do they support the California government launching an official blue ribbon panel to validate or invalidate the concept, to examine if this bold future for California is realistically possible, and to coordinate the array of details that such a change would entail? It is far beyond the scope of one person to write a book about that. That subject can only be written about by a "cloud," to use the Internet's terminology, so this book only attempts to pique curiosity at the mass public and governmental level and to start research.

II.

The unstated theme of this book is the difference between two beliefs about the best format for a society. These two beliefs have existed apart and confronted each other throughout the entire modern era—since the end of the Renaissance. One says that homogeneity, everyone acting and thinking alike and holding the same philosophies, is best. The other is the polar opposite: that diversity of people, opinion, action, thought, philosophy, expression, all held at the same time, is the optimum situation a society can obtain. The first belief sees that societies of great diversity have trouble reaching decisions and organizing resources from everyone for a common cause, and therefore are much slower in acting as a society to address specific problems and dynamic changes. The other belief, while agreeing that a diverse society loses some speed in enacting solutions, maintains that whatever speed is lost in not being homogenous is gained back one hundred to one thousand times in ability to fully appreciate all of the dimensions of problems that societies face. According to this view, such a society takes advantage of the full extent of opportunities that are available because of change, and the ability to look at all options for solving any problem. In other words, the ability to see things in their full dimension and to be able to see all totally new ways that a society could consciously evolve itself to a new plateau of existence—abilities that are simply not attainable in homogeneous societies. California exemplifies this second concept as a living thing, currently and in the past and, because of these dynamics, forever into the future. Few places in the world practice this second belief, although many profess to. Fewer places have practiced this in the past. And few places, likely in the future, will be able to or even want to practice this other belief. While the world is becoming more democratic, it is becoming equally more xenophobic, as attested to by many UN reports. Democracy does not equal diversity, neither does capitalism, as many have hoped. Hitler's Germany, Mussolini's Italy, and modern Russia, China, Hungary, Germany, Italy, France, Switzerland, Mexico, and Thailand all were or are democracies with capitalist economies, and all have shown or are showing their distaste for diversity, just to name a handful of examples.

III.

The world is changing dramatically in key ways, will fundamentally shift the global balance of power. These shifts in power are unstoppable, their time has come, and they will be as dramatic as the global rearrangement of power that happened from 1940–1950 when entirely new players were demoted in power and others raised to new heights. Because of this unstoppable change, America is in a delicate situation where it has to compete on a level playing field with new competitive and equally large peers in a way it fundamentally has never had to. Historical baggage is holding America back from moving ideologically into a new role to better fit this new era. But America can undertake dramatic change now, just as it has in the past. The steps that will remake the foundation of America's position to the world are laid out below. To my knowledge, this is the only book that lists all of the problems that America is facing and proposes an actual solution to them. Not a partial solution to only some of the problems, but a full one, that if enacted, although pricey, would place America in new house that will last through the storms of the next century. These changes are radical because the problems are dramatic, and tepid solutions don't have enough force to impact them in a meaningful way.

CALIFORNIA'S NEXT CENTURY 2.0

Part of the solution is for America to recognize both that the world needs a new facilitator of global dialogue and leadership and that in order for it to work best for this new era, America cannot be the one to provide it. Working with the power that it has now, America can create the new mechanisms of global facilitation just as it did after WWII with the UN, IMF, and other organizations, but it has to create someone or something else to act this role. Only an independent actor will gain the trust of the world needed to make the world a network of communication that can stand up to the dramatic and fast changes that will happen in the world over the next fifty years and beyond. By delicately placing someone else in the role of global nexus, America can secure world peace everywhere and secure its place as a leading power, determining the world's future regardless of what storms and

changes will come over the next one hundred years

of human evolution. This book is a plan for how

America can achieve all of these things by

embracing California to, literally, be all that it can

be.

CALIFORNIA'S NEXT CENTURY 2.0

CHAPTER 1: AMERICA'S GLOBALLY WEAK POSITION AND HOW TO FIX IT

WHEN YOU LOOK AT A MAP OF THE NATIONS OF THE ENTIRE WORLD, it doesn't appear that there is any order—but there is. And understanding or "seeing" that global order is the key to world peace and prosperity.

America's position in the world is in peril. Before WWII America was not a major player on the world stage, mostly only in Latin America. Since being the main wall against the expansion of communism from WWII to 1985 and the fall of the Berlin Wall, America has become known as the main country fighting for the preservation of capitalism and democracy. This created an impression of America across every nation in the world. When the Cold War ended, most of the nations that were not communist thought well of America for helping them fight communism, and most that were communist felt a closeness to America because it had been right about the economic and political system to have and was one of the friendliest victor nations in all of human history. However, in the last decade, the impression of America across the world has turned from positive to negative, and now a global phenomenon of fear and distrust of America has spread to almost every nation that had a positive image of America before. It has become globally popular not to trust or like America. The War in Iraq and the Global War on Terror, placed on top of pre-existing distrust of America in areas of Southeast Asia and Latin America, have created a runaway effect.

This is not an embellishment.

Two studies conducted by Princeton University have documented the economic costs of this dramatically increased anti-Americanism: "The Economic Impact of Anti-Americanism" by Nusrat Choudhury and "Anti-Americanism: A Clinical Study" by Bernard Chazelle. A McDonald's restaurant was destroyed in Ecuador, India has entertained calls for boycotts of American tobacco, beverages and cosmetics, and Germany has had restaurants voluntarily ban the sale of any American products. In a 2002 global poll, a majority of the people in thirty-four of forty-three countries said they disliked America's influence. Anti-Americanism is the most talked about form of anti-nationalism on the planet according to Internet traffic. Chazelle concludes, "Never has the United States been so alienated from the rest of the world."

A 2003 survey found that two-thirds of the world's countries felt more of an increased closeness to their own culture than to American culture, with some of the largest increases in this sentiment in traditional US allies of Japan, Turkey, and Indonesia. A 2005 global survey indicated that one-fifth of the planet's population specifically would not buy American products as a way of protesting (this survey was conducted one week after America helped with the Indonesian Tsunami relief). The survey also found that nearly 40% of the global population bases their opinion of America on its foreign policy alone, and that only 3% of the global population bases their opinion of America based on its products alone. In 2003, foreign travel to America dropped 30% from 2000 while world travel rose 40%, an almost inverse percentage in the amount of people traveling abroad but avoiding America. In 2008, an article entitled "The American Diaspora" said foreign travel to America was still 20% lower than before the Iraq War. In 2002, the world survey organization Pew Research Center conducted the "What the World Thinks in 2002" survey. It found that only half of South Koreans (America's traditional ally) had a positive opinion of America, only 1/3 of Chinese did, and only 9% of people in Turkey (another traditional American ally) did. Pew conducted another global survey in

2005 and found that anti-American opinion had only increased. Only 30% of the population of traditional American allies Germany and France had a positive opinion of America; 60% of England had a positive opinion. Less than one-third of the population of the different nations of Latin America had a positive opinion of America. Overall, Pew surveys from their Global Attitudes Project have found a substantial drop in opinion of America. An international tourism survey found that North American tourism growth is below Central American and less than half the growth of tourism in South America currently. In their book *America Against the World: How We Are Different and Why We Are Disliked* (2006), Andrew Kohut and Bruce Stokes conducted an unprecedented survey of world opinion and found that 70% of the world does not trust America as the sole superpower and thinks that the country is arrogant and warlike. One of America's most expert foreign policy advisors, Zbigniew Brzezinski, wrote a book in 2012, *Strategic Vision: America and the Crisis of Global Power*, aimed at attributing a significant portion of America's giant shift in loss of global appeal on two wars in the Middle East that did not grab the world's support. Foreign investment in America has been halved from 41% in 1999 to 18% in 2009, according to Global FDI.[1] China's foreign investment didn't drop until 2011, three years into the recession, and it only decreased 10%. In 2009,

---

[1] "US FDI Inflows Continue to Fall, President's Jobs Council to Recommend Ways to Reverse Trend," Global FDI, http://www.globalfdipost.com/content.php?530-US-FDI-Inflows-Continue-to-Fall-President-s-Jobs-Council-to-Recommend-Ways-to-Reverse-Trend, accessed October 9, 2011.

foreign investment in EU grew 10%. Mark Weisbrot of the Center for Economic and Policy Research stated, "I can't think of a time when the US has been more isolated."[2]

In addition to policy choices by America that have created this phenomena, this overall dynamic has been multiplied by another dynamic, America being the victim of its own success. When the world was broken up into communist and capitalist blocs, all of the world that did not want to be communist needed to work with America, the main power able to stand against and hold up the wall against Russia's central communist force. With America's defeat of Russia came a global acceptance that America had it right, that

---

[2] Nusrat Choudhury, "The Economic Impact of Anti-Americanism" (working paper, Princeton University, 2005).

democracy and capitalism are the way to run a modern nation. Now that every nation has this philosophy (even officially communist nations have elections and practice free market economic policies), countries don't need to partner with America and prefer to create their own sphere where they are the dominant power, essentially the America in their own backyards, for political and national pride reasons. It works for new powers to let America fade away because it means they can grow to fill in the power vacuum, making themselves stronger. Schadenfreude is the name of this concept: where you don't hurt the other party, but you are very happy to see them fall and shrink. Half of this dynamic is because of direct policy choices by America; the other half is because of the logical conclusion to the only side that America could have taken in the global war for "end of history" capitalism and democracy or dictatorship and government-run economies. Either way, and most likely because both phenomena exist at the same time, America's era as the leader of the world is shrinking in scope. As new superpowers rise to the same size economically as America over the next three decades, leading up to a predicted height at 2040, America's sphere of influence, number of allies, and financial resources to influence the world will continue to shrink. It's not that America is weakening but that the days of it being the only good guy in town are over. Now at least five other players equally capable of doing everything America can do will ride into the same small town—what is referred to as "the rise of the rest."

These other players are capitalizing on America's poor position in the world to create a future where America is pushed out of most of the regions of the world where it currently has an impressionable position and much global trade in. China is funding countries America will not and building a navy to challenge America's. China literally told America and India to stay out of the entire southern China Sea and surrounding area that belongs to nearly ten different countries. They have positioned themselves to great success in the last decade as the specific alternative to America. They are the "not America" option for countries who want massive foreign investment, expertise, and support at world bodies. Many countries have jumped at the service, often turning away from America after they have made deals with China.

India recently, in 2005, bested America at Air Force war games and this year, 2012, turned down a large military contract for US industries after taking American nuclear technology in a trade deal. China and the new rising superpowers are working together to remove the dollar from international transactions so that they can lock out America from being involved in all world trade.[3] Mercosur is not so much about trade between Latin America but creating a political organization that can keep America out.[4] FTAA was a plan led by America to extend NAFTA; Latin America rejected the whole

---

[3] Francis Marion Nation, "Now They Are Throwing B.R.I.C.S." *Dancing Czars* (blog), www.dancingczars.wordpress.com.

[4] Joanna Klonsky and Stephanie Hanson, "Mercosur: South America's Fractious Trade Bloc," The Council on Foreign relations, August 20, 2009.

thing.[5] ASEAN rejects American demands for action on human rights.[6] US officials were not at an ASEAN meeting.[7] Shanghai Cooperation Organization is the world's largest regional security organization center, and it excludes America.[8] What can America do to retain its leadership in the world that it has held since 1945? It can retain its

---

[5] Claudio Katz, "FTAA at Global Exchange" and "FTAA—Illusion and Reality." Global exchange (Blog), accessed May 3 2012, http://www.globalexchange.org/resources/ftaa. Claudio Katz is an economist and researcher. He is a fellow at the International Institute for Research and Education, in Amsterdam, and a teacher at the University of Buenos Aires. Katz is involved in the Argentine network "Economistas de Izquierda" (EDI).

[6] Agence France-Presse, "ASEAN Rejects Call to Expel Myanmar: Thai PM," July 23, 2009.

[7] Agence France-Presse, "US-ASEAN Economic Ties 'Priority' Despite No-Show."

[8] David C. Speedie, "Good Neighbors? The Shanghai Cooperation Organization," *Carnegie Council,* February 18, 2010.

global leadership position, but it will have to evolve, dramatically and drastically. But this evolution must not come about with any greater scale or effort than the dramatic change America underwent from 1930 to 1950 when it went from one of the world's lesser players associated only with smaller areas of the world (a junior partner to multiple European nations) to being the largest power in the world with interests across the entire planet. But this time without any actual loss of life or actual fighting. That change that Americans, some who live today, undertook was dramatic and quick, but it happened because Americans understood the way the world worked and the stakes in not maintaining a certain global order, and they simply stepped up to the challenge.

The world is changing in ways that America cannot stop. It's essentially inevitable. However, with direct shifts in its global presence and the formation of its nation, America can retain its global leadership for the next one hundred years. America is in serious trouble, not because of its own fault but because of a collection of events beyond its control. It is in the middle of a "super perfect storm."

A perfect storm is when two different storms come together and hit a ship from two different directions; America is in the middle of eight different storms all converging.

Storm One. America is in its highest debt since the Civil War, higher than WWII—a debt that could take thirty years to get out of.

CALIFORNIA'S NEXT CENTURY 2.0

Storms Two and Three. America has been lagging along since 1970 with 25% of its economy missing. In the 1980s, America's dollar began to lose power to the rising economies of countries that were destroyed during WWII. Instead of re-growing the industrial base to compete in the new world order, America decided to take out loans and go into massive debt as individual consumers and as a government to buy more nondurable "consumer" goods. This spending on cheap, disposable American products did boost the economy but only as the amount of debt grew. In the late 1990s to 2000s, America's credit was reaching massive proportions of global debt. In order to fill into the continuing 25% of the lost economy, America grew the financial services sector, or stock market trading, with looser regulations and new products, trading money that was already created and accounted for 25% of the US economy before the recession. This gigantic amount of the economy that was based on money speculation is what caused the American recession today. Now with the stock market hurt, and not fulfilling its 25% of the economy and no more ability to take out loans, there is nothing to replace the lost 25% from the 1970s.

Storm Four. Most of the infrastructure of America was built during the "New Deal era" from 1930 to the late 1960s. All of the airports, seaports, roads, schools, public buildings, and electrical infrastructure were created during this time, and all of it with a twenty-five to thirty-five year design life. All of the nation's infrastructure should have been replaced in 1980, when it was at 100% of its design life. Instead America spent its credit on nondurable goods and didn't build infrastructure. Then in the 1990s up through 2010, America's infrastructure was at 200% of its design life; and now the country is in a recession that will take decades to get out of just to reach the state America was in the early 1980s. By that time, all of America's infrastructure (which every modern economy depends on to run as a competitive economy) will be at 300% of its design life. Only central Africa and India have infrastructure that is this old and still used, and their globally recognized worst performance rates show what will happen.

Storm Five. The world is shifting, and new global power players are rising, some of whom will have economies as large as America and who don't want America to have influence in their region of the globe. At the same time that America is least able to compete globally due to poor infrastructure, the most powerful competition arises.

Storm Six. Global recession occurs that weakens the strength of all economies and puts them into debt just to keep their economy afloat. Some estimates suggest it will take ten years for America to naturally emerge from the recession.

Storm Seven. America is currently involved in two wars that are not over and that have run for nearly ten years: Iraq and Afghanistan. America's commitment to winning in these wars may continue to require serious resources for another ten to twenty years, creating a massive bill when America has no more credit and is struggling to deal with recession.

Storm Eight. America's global reputation is the worst it has been in the last century, during a time when there are real options to challenge its leadership.

The empires of Rome and England came down due to perfect storms, the combining of two giant storms—massive wars that they had to fight and an economic system that no longer brought in massive wealth. These simple perfect storms brought down the two mightiest empires before America; how will America deal with eight combined storms?

CALIFORNIA'S NEXT CENTURY 2.0

If America doesn't do something quick and truly radical, it is entirely likely that it will stay economically weak for another thirty years, as multiple players rise to become wealthier than it and create a new world order where America is excluded or her participation strongly downplayed. This would create a condition like the one in Spain at the end of the 1800s, an empire in name that who was easily toppled by a nation much younger and still not that powerful. America should know this scenario well for it was America that recognized the situation of Spain in 1890 and so easily toppled her entire global empire within just three years.

Where's the leadership? Where are the new plans? The way forward? The big change that America is going to do to change and ingenuity to adapt like in 1812, 1860, 1945, 1965? It appears that it is not there. No leader or intellectual in America has suggested anything to remove America from this storm system other than repeating more of the same old ideas—get government out of regulating business, tax the super wealthy, return to our traditional values of ingenuity, have faith in the family. It appears that there are no new ideas but only repeats of bland slogans. As a well-established foreign policy journalist said in 2012, "The foreign-policy theme that should dominate this year's presidential campaign is 'American renewal.' Each candidate claims to have a strategy for halting the nation's decline, but their versions often amount to 'more of the same'—which isn't going to work."[9]

---

[9] David Ignatius, "Foreign Policy Thinking Is Thin This US Election Year," *The Daily Star*, January 26, 2012.

The Advisory Commission on Public Diplomacy's 2005 Report suggested doing more traditional outreach.[10] The Heritage Foundation, a conservative think tank, in a lecture entitled "Anti-Americanism and Responses to American Power," recommended several actions the US should undertake — including work more with allies to fight terrorism. The Policy Coordinating Committee on Public Diplomacy and Strategic Communication led by the under secretary for Public Diplomacy and Public Affairs recently published the US National Strategy for Public Diplomacy and Strategic Communication in June 2007—it recommended an increase in education and exchange programs and aid to

---

[10] http://www.state.gov/r/adcompd/rls/55903.htm.

countries, and to act on more traditional outreach.[11] The article admits that to get out of the recession, it will take ten years and multiple decades to shift to a new form of economy for the next era, but it offers that the main thing to do now is not to panic and for economists to make people feel better about the economy so they will invest. Another suggestion is that the government just needs to spend even more money to get out of the recession.[12]

Fareed Zakaria the foreign policy analyst, offers this: The solution is to cut massive federal programs, massively invest in education, massively invest in infrastructure, allow massive more

---

[11] Quentin Fottrell, "10 Things Economists Won't Tell You: Why Their Forecasts Should Be Taken With a Shaker Of Salt," *Smartmoney.com*, August 24, 2011.

[12] Clyde Prestowitz, "Bretton Woods Outlook Dark for America," *Foreign Policy,* April 13, 2011.

immigrants to stay and take domestic jobs,

constantly compare what America doesn't do as

well as other countries, aka more of the same.[13]

Later, Zakaria says that real problem is that

America doesn't want honest politicians who will

be honest with them about where America stands in

relation to other countries, which is again another

long-heard suggestion going back decades.[14] Other

solutions call for American citizens and their

government representatives to be careful what they

say when they are abroad.[15] "Rebooting America's

Image Abroad" by Walter R. Roberts (Public

---

[13] Fareed Zakaria, "How to Restore the American Dream," *Time,* October 21, 2010.

[14] Ibid, "Are America's Best Days Behind Us?" *Time*, March 3, 2011.

[15] Melvin L. Sharpe, "America's international image problem—Mass Media," *USA Today*, July 2002.

Diplomacy Alumni Association) reviews

government efforts to improve public opinion and

says that the main improvement would be having a

foreign communications position who directly

reports to the president just as there is a secretary of

Defense and of State. "How to Fix the Economy:

An Expert Panel" by Tom Keene (Bloomberg

Businessweek, 2010) says that politicians need to be

better at working together and entitlements have to

be drastically removed. What is worse than only

repeating all old ideas instead of formulating

something new for a unique situation the likes of

which America has never faced before, is that some

foreign policy thinkers argue that the problem is not

that bad and is mostly media exaggeration for the

sake of news.[16] Former vice president and foreign

---

[16] Sam Norton, *Beyond Celebrity: How Obama Can Remake*

policy expert Dick Cheney said that there wasn't an image problem at all.[17] But also, the federal government authored a study by twenty top foreign policy experts who concluded that the problem was not that bad and that President Obama had already significantly improved the image problem.[18] One year later, an official survey of the Muslim world showed the collection of American academics was

---

America's Image (Princeton University: American Foreign Policy, 2009), http://afpprinceton.com/2009/12/beyond-celebrity-how-obama-can-remake-america%e2%80%99s-image/. See also David Von Drehle, "Don't Bet Against the United States," *Time*, March 3, 2011.

[17] Saul Relative, "Cheney on 'Today': Believes Iraq War Did Not Hurt US Reputation," *Yahoo contributor network,* August 30, 2011, http://contributor.yahoo.com/user/133651/saul_relative.html.

[18] Peter Katzenstein and Jeffrey Legro, "Think Again: America's Image," Foreign Policy, October 5, 2009, http://www.foreignpolicy.com/articles/2009/10/05/think_again_americas_image.

wrong and that America's popularity in the Muslim world had declined even further since he was president.[19] Furthermore, at a conference of supporters, President Obama told people who were seriously distressed about America's position in the world and its deficit to simply "stop complaining." **This isn't an original conclusion,** scholars in foreign policy have stated it as well:

> "Too many American leaders—both in government and corporate are gripped by denial, a type of Pollyanna group-think that insists that America will retain its greatness no matter what."[20]

---

[19] Ronald Kessler, "Obama's Muslim Outreach Fails," Newsmax, July 20, 2010; Louis Navellier, "How To Fix The US Deficit," Forbes.com, May 3, 2010.

[20] James Canton, *The Extreme Future: The Top Trends That Will Reshape the World in the Next 20 Years*, (Dutton adult, 2006), 36.

"Unfortunately, American firms and the American government are showing signs of being more concerned about yesterday's innovations than about creating tomorrow's."[21]

"One of the problems with the United States over the last generation is that Americans haven't felt there was much to learn from the rest of the world because America was so dominant and English a more or less universal language. The world has changed, but Americans haven't yet caught up."[22]

---

[21] Michael Porter, *Competitive Advantage of Nations* (New York: the Free Press, 1990), 727.

[22] Francis Fukuyama, "Democracy Still Rules. But Will US Catch Up in a Changing World?" *Christian Science Monitor*, June 8 2011.

CALIFORNIA'S NEXT CENTURY 2.0

Surveying the discussion in America suggests that among the public in general and the experts, the problem is not perceived as being that serious and is easily fixable by returning to old solutions. The reality as described above, with the eight storms closing in on America, is quite different.

This book presents the only plan (the only one proposed at this time, it appears) that could realistically improve America's image abroad dramatically (by signaling its continuing commitment to freedom), secure its influence for the future (by having California linked to America and being the new nexus for global negotiation), and reduce the debt to a manageable level within ten years (by increasing American tax revenue by one-third without requiring any services for the money).

CALIFORNIA'S NEXT CENTURY 2.0

The eight storms mentioned before, will require the four steps below to confront:

1. Allow the very few sizable Native American populations within America (the Five Civilized Tribes, Navajo, Lakota, Blackfeet, and possibly Chippewa) and the very few territories that had existing governments before they were joined with America (Hawaii, Puerto Rico, California, Guantanamo Bay), all of whom were conquered by military force and forced to join the American union from the beginning—to be returned to independent state status in a fair vote. (If they choose not to become independent in that vote, then they stay as a territory or state, but it would be globally documented that the freedom to choose was allowed.) Most of this land is in areas where the overwhelming

majority of the American population does not live, greatly reducing the impact. This public relations "event" will equal the famed Marshall Plan in the scope and power of a positive public image across the entire world after WWII. That event set such a platform of trust and goodwill across the entire world with its inspiring image of goodness that the following era became known as the "Pax Americana." It will be comparable to the international impact of seeing America as a beacon of liberty to the developing world—the one John Kennedy spoke of in his 1963 Civil Rights speech announcing a new day for minorities in America.

Currently all of the plans that have been proposed and tried by all of the greatest minds on how to improve America's world image have not been shown to work. The current president's reaching out to the Muslim world, one-fifth of the planet's population, has not been shown to improve global impressions. The situation is to the point where the American government has accepted the "new global reality" and is actively working not to attach its name to major international legislation and projects because it knows it will increase the chances of other nations agreeing to work with the action. "Leading from behind" has become the new catchphrase of America's foreign policy.

This plan, unlike any other proposed, will set a solid platform for trust with the world and from where America can re-launch an improved public image that will last for decades or another century the way the Marshall Plan did for America at the start of the 1950s. A few key independence movements will be enough to catch the world's attention. The possibility of Puerto Rican independence captured the attention of all of Latin America, as proved by the attendance at the Latin American and Caribbean Congress in Solidarity with Puerto Rico's Independence held in Panama in 2006. England has recognized the case for independence in its main newspaper, the *Telegraph*, for both Hawaii and California, and Russia has recognized the case for California. The largest forum of all Asian nations, APEC, was held in Hawaii in 2011, bringing the role of Hawaii in America to all of Asia's attention.

2. Use these new states along with an increased
   formal effort for American emigration to
   countries with already existing substantial
   American populations to create an American
   Diaspora empire, as already practiced by
   France, England, Russia, India, and China in
   this new era of fully global trade. All major
   superpowers except for America and Brazil
   already have formal policies where they are
   using their Diaspora as a way to secure
   economic, political, cultural, and information
   "beachheads" in major sections of the world
   economy. This is "the new way to empire."
   America will literally have to follow these other
   nations and begin to makes its own New
   American Empire. The new nation states made
   from America, although different from the

average American state, will be American like in their mindset. Along with other independent nations having a strong American presence increased by American emigration, the new nation states will project the American mindset to the world, continuing America's global leadership but as a friend standing side by side, rather than an overbearing father figure (an unpopular image to any nation that considers itself an economic or cultural equal). And this event will allow America to compete as all of the other major superpowers of the future, except for Brazil, do. Currently America has no plan to undertake any effort to capitalize on its existing Diaspora, and the American government is seen by Americans living abroad as viewing them as a "liability instead of an asset."

3. Make one of these newly created states serve the role that Switzerland did in the last 150 years: as the global negotiations and trade nexus for the new world order that is currently being developed. The world is changing, and new powers are rising to the same level as America, and nothing can be done to stop this. Understand that the new world powers are challenging all traditional centers of world negotiation because they are seen as created and controlled by American and European powers— and even to Europe as mostly American controlled. New powers are making their own leagues of dialogue and trade and are outright forbidding America to join, or severely limiting

its presence to the side bench of negotiations, in an attempt to secure their own area of the planet and hold the amount of power and influence that America once held in that arena. Nothing can be done to stop this situation. Old institutions of negotiation, such as the UN, IMF, World Bank, WTO, G20, are based on voluntary partnership; no one can force a nation to join or to take the effort seriously or to make their own organizations that do the exact same thing. However, America can permanently retain an American mindset in the global leadership discussions and a physical presence at the negotiation table by allowing an American like nation to be become the New Switzerland for the next century, filling the role of a living UN. Just as Switzerland was the world negotiation and business hub for over a century from the early 1800s to the 1940s, a new hub could be created, one that because of its history, is American like in thinking, securing America's position in all global affairs and securing American philosophies in world development everywhere.

4. Keep doing what America is doing; keep working on all of the other fronts. Currently this is the only goal. And it seems to be holding America in place, but only maybe (the future is uncertain), and possibly only holding it—or slowing its shrinking—is much like Hadrian's Wall during the last days of the Roman Empire. However, with these three other policy grand moves, on top of America's current policy, the

combined force of public relations image and new directions of embracing the global economy will throttle America up and over its current problems.

These steps will require radical moves by the American government, but nothing that will affect the average American very much at all frankly.

Achieving Step 1. Less than 5% of the land that Americans actually live on, where the overwhelming majority of the American population exists, will go to the creation of new states (essentially just the new tribal lands in Oklahoma). And there will be no loss economically for a couple of reasons. First is that all business deals and commerce negotiations between the new countries and America will stay the same as it is today. This is because of the unique form of independence that all of these states will undertake, that of "sub-national sovereignty," which we'll cover later. Most of the native territories only receive money from the American government and don't generate much income, so there will not be an income loss from these areas. The territories that aren't native do produce some money, but California and Hawaii have large amounts of federal land that require maintenance money from the federal government and have many native reservations that also only absorb federal money. Furthermore, California and Hawaii are 14% of the population but only 11% of the US economy, meaning that together they need more money for their populations than they actually produce economically. Puerto Rico is a net receiver of American financial assistance. Additionally, all of the new nations will be much more focused on international trade than they ever were when part of America because of slowness in passing trade laws at the federal level and because, being small, these nations will have to compete globally. Increasing in trade but being connected to America means increased international trade with America.

Achieving Step 2.. America will have to make it easier for Americans to work and live abroad, which means changing the tax code for Americans abroad—not the rest of the country—no more than 5% of the population. However, the increase in world trade will more than cover any loss in a small percentage of the population. Americans will have to be more open to world news and pay more attention to world tastes, but they won't have to go to school to do this, just be more open in their daily lives.

Achieving Step 3. America does not have to stop working with the UN, IMF, World Bank, and all other institutions. They will continue, as the world will have multiple negotiation nodes even if it has a new hub; rather America will simply have to not stop a new hub from forming. The nation that becomes this new hub—fulfills the role to the world of the "new Switzerland for the next century"—will do all of the work in establishing themselves as a hub because they will have to in order to establish their legitimacy through independence.

For a very small investment of land, and no net economic loss, America's image can grow to its original world high state, truly and deeply inspiring the world with its love of freedom. America will be in a position to compete the way all of the new superpowers of the world are going to compete with the new form of empire. America's seat at the table at world negotiations will be secured directly, and an American philosophy about world development will be secured indirectly.

CHAPTER 2: AMERICA'S NEW MAP FOR THE NEXT CENTURY

Story 1:

Righting all of the wrongs so that the nation can be seen as starting fresh and clean.

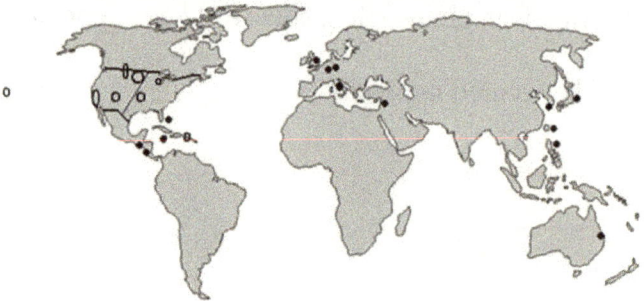

Circles = new states

Dots = American presence

The future?

CALIFORNIA'S NEXT CENTURY 2.0

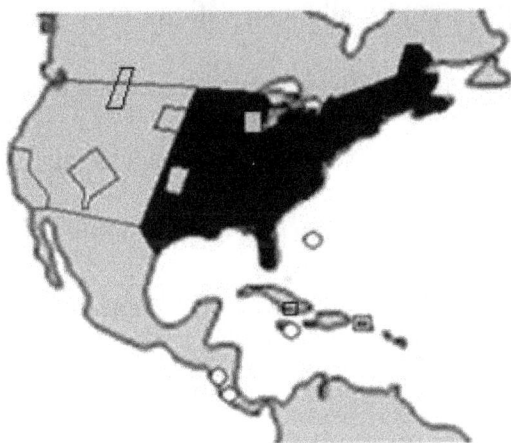

In order to create a public relations event that will shock the entire world with its love and last in the minds of all of the world's population for multiple generations, America will undo all of the wrongs that it has committed in the past on American soil—to the degree that is realistically feasible. Just as the world was shocked by the goodwill and generosity of America after WWII—when they neither took everything of value from the nations that they had conquered nor subjugated their people to serfdom (as was the pattern for all major nations, even in Europe, up to this time)—but instead enacted the Marshall Plan, so too will the world react to this great event.[1] America again will enact a public relations action that will be as equal a game change in the way all modern nations act for the future of world history. America will release those Native American nations with dense enough populations to run an effective government and those sections of land that were taken away from an existing government for the sake of military conquest, attempting to undo 150 years of wrong history.

---

[1] With the Marshall Plan, America said with deeds, in a message that the entire world talked about to themselves, that they would spend their own American money to build up the nations that had attacked them because they thought it was the right thing to do, and because they wanted a future of equality and peace and not subjugation, even if they did have the right.

CALIFORNIA'S NEXT CENTURY 2.0

Canada gained world attention in the late 1990s and
influenced England and America on major domestic
policy (some experts have argued this was the first
time in history) when it recognized the wrongful
taking of native land and officially apologized at the
highest levels of government in the most public
address possible. Before this Canada didn't lead
other English-speaking nations in anything and was
not talked about on the world stage; this one event
made a gigantic shift.

**The consequences of four steps mentioned
before, are discussed further below.**

**1. America, where the main population actually
lives, only loses a small amount of land, three-**

quarters of Oklahoma for the Five Civilized Tribes.

The rest of the new nations are taken from land that Americans don't really live on—the Lakota Nation would absorb half of North Dakota, the Navajo Nation would absorb the four corners of Arizona, New Mexico, Utah, and Colorado, as well as a land bridge to the other Navajo reservations not currently connected at Fort Apache and San Carlos in Arizona. The Blackfeet reservation would double in size in Montana, and America would work with Canada to link it to the Blackfeet reservation just inside the Canadian border. The Chippewa, if they are willing to consolidate their scattered reservations into one giant piece about a one-fifth of northern Minnesota (an area few Americans live in because of the extreme cold), could also gain independence. However, none of these areas are places where the main American population (MAP) lives. American populations in these states mentioned above live in cities located near these native areas but not in them.

2. Hawaii, California, Puerto Rico, and Guantanamo Bay in Cuba would be released because they were taken by military assault against the original inhabitants' will.

America has already established a precedent for this by releasing first Cuba and then the Philippines because it recognized that it was a historical wrong to hold on to these countries taken by military conquest. And only a few years ago, President

Clinton acknowledged that it was wrong for America to take Hawaii. British and Russian scholars have already noted that American policy of support for Kurdistan, Croatia, and South Sudan is in direct conflict with America's holding of California, given its past.

The concept that a global image makeover can occur from simply giving back small pieces of land has already been postulated by research based at America's oldest and most prestigious university: Harvard. Professor Jonathan Hansen has argued that simply giving back Guantanamo to Cuba, for example, would signal a new era in equal relations with America to the entire Latin American southern hemisphere. This small measure on its own would be enough to "lay the groundwork for a new

foundation with Latin America" on its own.[2]

It is key to acknowledge that America will not

disintegrate. The country will lose about 10% of its

landmass, but rather only about 4% of the land

where Americans actually live. The overall gigantic

size of America, which reaches from "sea to shining

sea," will still stay intact. This will not be the

disintegration of America that other nations have

predicted. It is important that no other American

nations will be able to leave. This program is a one-

time event, not an open tunnel for other states to

---

[2] Jonathan Hansen, *Guantanamo: An American History* (New York: Hill and Wang, 2011). It should also be noted that the author points out in the book that military leaders have said that the loss of Guantanamo would pose no risk to US military preparedness, and that the island is not held onto for any security reasons.

leave. Because of the legal precedent under which this action is taking place, only nations with a pre-existing government taken against their will, will be returned. This does not apply to any other American state. Furthermore, not all American territories and Native Lands will be returned because their populations are simply too small to run an effective country and would be reduced to the standard of living of the independent states of Swaziland in South Africa (among the poorest and most corrupt in the entire planet). Allowing countries like that to exist does no one any good. Native areas suggested above are limited to a population of one hundred thousand and the ability to live on one landmass. Permitting sovereign nations below this amount would be unworkable. Therefore there are only a few Native American populations that qualify.

Furthermore none of the new nations will become fully independent, but rather sub-nationally sovereign as Scotland is to England, or "mostly completely independent." This is explained in more detail later in the book.

Let's examine the economic shock related to this plan. California and Hawaii contribute as much to the US economy as they are a percentage of the population: 12.5% of the population and 13% of the economy for California and .5% of the population and economy for Hawaii. Their removal from the US economy results in no net gain or loss. In addition the federal government wouldn't have to pay for services for 13% of the population and would lose almost 13% of the economy. Furthermore, almost half of the land in California is locked into federal reserve lands, meaning lands that are unable to be turned into profit for private business. Whereas for most of the main population of America, all of the land is able to be sold for private use and therefore used for profit. In fact, the amount of federal reserve land in MAP is roughly equal to all of the federal land just in the state of California alone. Puerto Rico and Guantanamo Bay are net receivers of federal funds, as are all of the Native American tribal lands. Besides creating new "American like" nations, Americans will emigrate to other nations with existing significant American populations and form new large American communities. America already has a Diaspora that Americans never discuss: nations that already have a large American population of citizens and businesses and are already used to American people and entertainment. America will capitalize on these areas and increase its population to the point that it is a sizable minority in this independent nation, creating a dynamic where that nation, although independent in many world forums, also "feels" America's concerns because they are part of its people. Americans would become substantial minorities in EL Salvador, Costa Rica, Jamaica, and Bermuda. Those nations with a more American mindset would form a region of more American sentiment with the new nations of Puerto Rico and the North Carolina native nations. Americans in Japan, Taiwan, South Korea, Australia, and the Philippines would influence those nations who would link with the new nation of Hawaii to project American values independent of America. And American populations in England, Germany,

CALIFORNIA'S NEXT CENTURY 2.0

France, Italy, and Israel would help ensure an American mentality in this region.

The American presence would be felt in Central America, throughout Asia, and northern Europe as American minority populations grow on existing American presence. Without even trying officially, as India, China, England, Russia, and France have done, America already has a global presence equal to or greater than these nations. If America actually formally made this a national objective by changing the tax codes, talking about the subject of American emigrants with pride, and the government formally sponsoring the effort with national politicians encouraging it with the same zeal they do American strength, it is most likely that America would excel beyond the abilities of all other major nations taking this policy.

Furthermore, this new form of empire is the way the world is going. World trade is the way that nations will rise to power and claim sections of the globe under influence, not military conquest. China, India, Russia, and Europe have all recognized this; the only major powers to not fully and consciously undertake this effort as a nation are America and Brazil. India has grown its home economy within just three years, increasing trade by 100%, by using its population abroad in the US to form connections between Indian people in the home country and America. Chinese overseas population is considered by some as the third largest economy in the world; it has been considered by American political economists to be one of the main reasons for the rapid growth of China. "Symptomatically, China's main vehicle for international dialogue about itself are the several hundred Confucius Institutes actively being established around the world, modeled on the French Alliance Française and the UK's British Councils."[3]

England's commonwealth of nations has one-third of the world's population, and through the Commonwealth Business Council, it works on increasing financial and trade links between all members, who comprise one-quarter of all world trade. The French have Organization Internationale de la Francophonie that works for improvement of economic governance of all members and the formation of common opinions on international issues. Russia has the Eurasian Economic Community, aimed at making a common market

---

[3] Zbigniew Brzezinski, *Strategic Vision: America and the Crisis of Global Power* (New York: Basic books, 2012), 180.

through continuing trade deals, inter-member
investment, and, eventually, a common dollar.
A new form of empire has many different terms:
"cultural imperialism" (in that the culture freely
chooses to embrace the foreign culture by
individual citizens who do so because they like it as
opposed to a foreign culture forced on a people),
"banal imperialism," "cultural diplomacy," or the
most currently used term, "soft power."

The truth is that America is going to have to
compete against the world on equal terms, playing
the same game that all of the other superpower
nations do. It will have to encourage Diaspora and
connect to it economically and culturally in order to
greater influence the world. The entire world is
going this way, and America will not be able to stop
or change the direction of human evolution.

Americans will create a pipeline for foreign ideas and business to come directly into the American mindset. Expatriates, through their family and friends and just participating in the American community, will bring new ideas into America that will make America more understanding of the world and thereby dramatically more able to compete as equals in the new-forming world order. Four percent of the American population will have to be okay with emigrating outside of America (a low percentage because of the giant size of the main American population), and 96% of Americans will only have to be more open to new ideas as the cost for enacting the new American empire. America has the strength and financial resources to make it profitable for nations to take on more Americans. Furthermore, the new nations indicated above that don't want to undertake independence don't have to. It will be put to a public vote with international monitors so that the world will verify that America gave these places the option and they turned it down to stay part of America of their own free will. America needs to do this because it has lost the role as the "shining city upon the hill." It used to be the country that promised democracy to the world's populations, but recently it has lost that inspirational role. The world is looking at other systems of democracy. Hong Kong and Macau so far like the SAR form of government of China. Tibet has asked to have China look into this form also, as has Taiwan. They have not asked for American-style federalism. Africa has formed the AU based on the EU form of democracy. The Middle East is looking into an Arab Union based on the EU also, not a federal system as in America. The USSR's member countries, which initially gravitated to America after the fall of the Cold War have gravitated back toward Russia in the last decade and have shown a willingness to enter into a Russian-centric EU-style community. Even the American nation state project of Iraq has chosen a parliamentary style of democracy similar to Europe rather than the winner-take-all style as in America. America's version of democracy is not as popular as it once was, and given a choice many parts of the world are choosing other forms of democracy. This act will grab people's attention of America's good will and prove their commitment to democracy and show that America is still the place that, with democracy, innovates successfully to new heights of human and industrial achievement.

FEDERAL VERSUS UNION GOVERNMENT

SYSTEMS

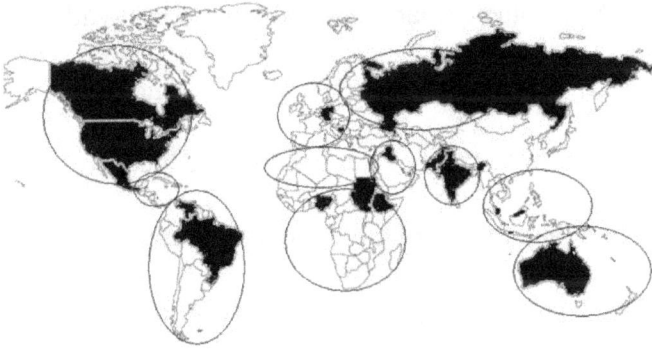

Shaded = American-style federated governments

(federal states)

Circle = European Union–style government

arrangements (trade blocs)

Nations of the world in Federal governments versus Union style governments

There is almost the same number of federal

governments as there are trade unions. Most of the

world is not in an American federal–style

government arrangement, but most of the world is

already part of a European style–trade union.
Federations and unions are not more complicated
than the other. A large federal government with
many powers given to the capital is complicated,
but one with most power given to the local areas is
not. However, all of the trade unions are large and
involve detailed agreements between each two
members states, making trade unions very
complicated and yet equally as popular as federal
systems.

**Federalism, the American-style march of
progress, is seriously challenged by the
European cultural model of a union.** Currently
the two systems championed by America and
Europe are roughly equally popular, with more of
the world choosing to follow and copy the European

model. Academics have also stated that it is likely the American style of union will be less popular in the future: "Heavy government intervention in national economies does not improve the functioning of markets, and the same applies to supranational institutions. In a more integrated world there will be a need for supranational institutions, financial and legal, but not for large federations of countries."[4]

America needs good, global-reaching PR that shows that its brand is better, more current, than all of the other brands out there. Rather than letting the image of America slide to its lowest point, now is the best time to start a PR campaign to

---

[4] Enrico Spolaore and Albert Alesina, *The Size of Nations* (MIT Press, 2005), 224.

restore America's image back to a high level and establish a presence so that it can maintain its standing at this global image plateau. This is how Scottish-style independence for California with America's blessing can fit in.

America used to wear the mantle as the high point, the shining beacon of democracy, showing the world how it could get many different people to work together. The global mantel for making democracy work and the world's attention are shifting from America (with the Patriot Act, violations of international law for the war on terror, extraordinary renditions, stripping of the Bill of Rights for legal citizens, legal kidnapping, torture) to Europe with the EU and China with Hong Kong. The EU is an impressive organization, able to have fair, democratic, open debates that bring together many different peoples who speak different languages. China has allowed Hong Kong to carry on almost completely as an independent country, and Hong Kong still thrives and attracts massive foreign tourists and investments. Both of these arrangements have caught the attention of the entire world—Taiwan and Tibet want to become sub-national governments to China like Hong Kong. The Middle East, Africa, South America, and South Asia are all looking into forming arrangements based closely on the EU model. The world is talking about Chinese- and European-"style" federalism—not American-style federalism.

When the entire globe was divided into two camps—democracy/freedom/capitalism and dictatorship/communism/state-controlled—about half of the world would agree with American ideas proposed at the UN or other world organizations because for sure they did not support the other side. Despite what George W. Bush said as president of America, the world is not with America or against it, it's looking around for other options and acting like informed consumers—picking what they want when and how they want it. And the world of smaller nations can do this because now there are five to seven big-box retailers instead of just one. America has a much harder time getting the world to sign onto its ideas. Iraq was one example, but Asian trade, Latin American trade, environmental protection, and human trafficking are all areas where America's ideas were rejected by the different regions. A significantly large reason for this is because it is popular for small nations to turn down a large giant. It's cool to snub your nose at America simply because America is so large. It's much how tiny sparrows in nature like to taunt giant eagles—just for fun. France is a perfect example of this. There are legitimate grievances, and then the leadership of these countries amplifies them to the maximum damaging extent they can be, largely for the pure point of entertainment. Because of America's image in the world today, small nations with only a few embarrassing facts can capture the negative attention of the entire world and focus it on America, a nation multiple times larger than they are.

Furthermore, releasing a gigantic nation (California being the world's fifth to eighth largest economy) would be seen as an enormous act of generosity, democracy, trust in federalism, in international partnership, and philanthropy. The fact that this doesn't happen very often, especially with a nation the size of California, would generate world publicity for at least two decades, if not five. In 1948 people were amazed that Israel was born, and it took about thirty years before it became old news. That's a high return on positive publicity during a time when America needs it more than ever. (America has never had this large an international presence and this large a negative world opinion, right or wrong, at the same time). America would regain its positive world reputation just as its reputation is at its lowest. Going into a time when there will be many other loud voices,

CALIFORNIA'S NEXT CENTURY 2.0

America would also grow even louder in its ability to have its arguments heard.

Adding to this global publicity event, America could gain even more global positive impression if it stated that it was also allowing California to do this for the sake of making a moral correction on a past deed, respecting both domestic and international law. California had an existing government, roads, infrastructure, when it was militarily taken over by America in 1850. Battles by native settlers were fought against the foreign invasion army and navy of America throughout northern, central, and southern California. American law has English common law as its base for its entire structure. America, Australia, New Zealand, and Canada were formed on the principle of "terra nullius" within English common law, which says that it is okay to claim an area if it is not developed. Hence why native lands were legally okay to be settled. Although morally wrong, the legal basis for America's existence still rests on this concept. In taking over California, America violated the basic tenet of law that allowed for it to exist in the first place. California was already marked out and mapped out, its property was divided, roads and infrastructure were built, and a working government was established. In addition it was defended by a formal army with different corps and officers. In fact, American military officers even remarked upon the dedication to the cause and valiance of the Californios. Only Hawaii and Louisiana can make the same argument of having been a developed area/country, with roads, infrastructure, cities, and a existing formal government. But America does not need to worry about expansion of the California concept to these two states because they would never be financially viable on their own—both depend on massive American investment and aid just to survive. (In all likelihood, a vote for independence by Hawaii would not happen because the state would have great difficulty maintaining the standard of living it has resting solely on its own local economy.)

Besides being contrary to the basis of domestic law, the claiming of territory gained with this sort of history, is also against international law and against the spirit of multiple American international interventions in the last two decades. A military organization from another country/group invaded an area and treated the local citizens as second-class people, murdered them, took their property, and removed their rights, even though they had a developed organized area. In Bosnia, Iraq, Afghanistan, and Sudan, America supported politically or got involved directly to fix what it internationally called an immoral situation. However, these actions are in a direct hypocritical contrast with how America gained California—and international organizations and bodies have noted this as such. While Americans may not be aware of this hypocrisy of law and precedent, the international community is. Publicly declaring a correction and seeking complete non-hypocrisy would gain even more positive global attention. Allowing some devolution will show that America is committed to federalism, which can keep the overall federal union healthy.[5]

Zbigniew Brzezinski wrote, "But to have the credibility and capacity…America needs to show the world that it has the will to renovate itself at home."[6]

Story 2:

Why would America allow California and a series of other small nations to leave? Doesn't this mean the dissolution and weakening of America?

---

[5] Michael S. Greve, *Real Federalism: Why It Matters, How It Could Happen*, (American Enterprise Institute, 1999); Enrico Spolaore and Albert Alesina, *The Size of Nations* (MIT press, 2005), ch. 9 and pg. 199; Paul Starobin, "Divided We Stand," *Wall Street Journal*, June 13, 2009.

[6] Zbigniew Brzezinski, *Strategic Vision: America and the Crisis of Global Power* (New York: Basic books, 2012), 185.

CALIFORNIA'S NEXT CENTURY 2.0

Modern powers have taken a cue from a very few small nations and realized that they have created a global empire through their Diaspora.

THE NEW WAY TO "EMPIRE"

Circles = France, Russia, England

Black dots = English

White squares = French

Black Sprinkles = Russian

Major powers and their language-based leagues

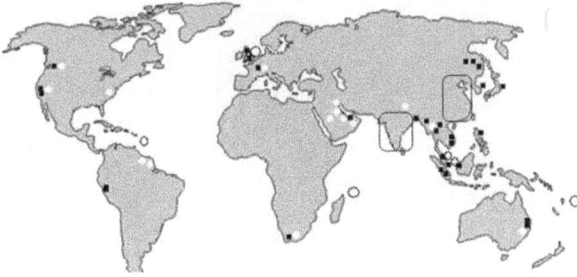

Ovals = China, India

Black squares = Chinese

White circles = Indian

Upcoming powers and their overseas Diasporas

Square = Israel

Black circles = Jewish communities

Square = Philippines

Black circles = Filipino communities

Square = Hungary

Black circles = Hungarian communities

Square = Turkey

Black circles = Turkic communities

Square: Switzerland

Black circles: Swiss populations

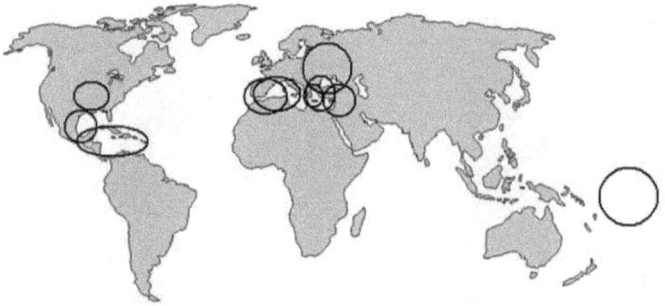

Areas of historical examples of new forms of empire

China and India have begun to reach out to their Diasporas in the last ten years. France and England moved to this strategy in the 1970s when they lost physical control of their former colonial empires; the idea was not to lose all of the value from running empires, so they wanted a link to them based on culture. Russia has focused on this strategy in the last ten years, once it realized that there was a new world economy based on trade deals and positive world television press. Of the future superpowers, only Brazil has not focused on its Diaspora.

These new states should be used along with an increased formal effort for American emigration to countries with pre-existing substantial American populations to create an American Diaspora empire. This is already practiced by France, England, Russia, India, and China in this new era of fully global trade. All major superpowers except for America and Brazil already have formal policies where they are using their Diaspora as a way to secure economic, political, cultural, and informational "beachheads" in major sections of the world economy.

Small nations have been using this strategy also. Turkey is reaching out to Turkic cultural communities throughout central Asia, eastern Europe, and Germany. The Philippines has made a special effort to expand emigrant workers and celebrate them as heroes returning home from destinations in the Persian Gulf, Asia, and California. Hungary has reached out to historic Hungarian populations in neighboring countries. Israel, perhaps the oldest nation state to follow this strategy, started in the 1950s with the beginning of Israel to reach out to historic Jewish communities around the world for trade and financial and cultural links. The Swiss government possibly has the best official Diaspora: official government posts have existed for decades helping the community to emigrate abroad and fully 10% of its population lives outside the country.

This form of recognizing the importance of emigrant communities far away from the home country came about because the world recognized that global trade is "the way" of the new world era and linking to other nations in strong ways improves the economic strength of the home nation. Exploding beyond the Israeli community in roughly more than the last ten years, the concept is not new and is linked to humans in general. Many ancient empires from around the world's cultures built themselves on establishing small colonies of their ethnic group throughout the region they traded with in order to establish better trade connections to the entire region. For example:

117

- the Varangians (the Vikings), specifically Sweden throughout eastern Russia, the Black Sea, and to Iran during their era, circa 1000 BC,

- Ancient Greeks in the eastern Mediterranean and Black Sea from 1000–700 BC

- the competitors of the ancient Greeks, the Phoenicians, around the same time, throughout the western Mediterranean, eventually becoming the Carthaginians who kept the same strategy against their competition during their era

- the Romans during the beginning of the Roman empire

- the Lapita, in Polynesia, 1300–300 BC

- the Swahili between East Africa's nations near Madagascar, 1000–1800 BC

- the Mycenaeans around Crete and southern Greece, 2000–1000 BC

- the Assyrians in Turkey and Syria, circa 1800 BC

- there is some evidence that this strategy was also used by the Olmec in central Mexico along the Gulf Coast, circa 1300–400 BC

- the Hopewell culture of Mississippi and Ohio based out of Cahokia,100–500 BC

- the ancient Maya around southern Mexico and Guatemala and the Caribbean islands, 300–600 BC

This may be the most natural way, as well as the most peaceful way, that humans have it in them to build empires.

EXISTING AMERICAN DIASPORA

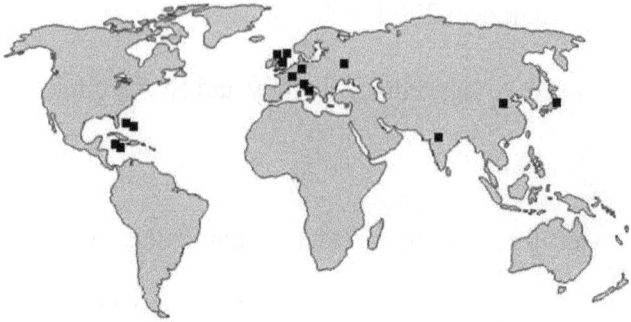

Black squares = current locations of major

American civilian presence

2011

Not well talked about in America, or barely

discussed at all, is the mass of Americans who are

moving overseas to stay. This is not including

Americans who routinely travel to other countries

for business, but people who grew up or have been

socialized in America who are moving to other

countries to put down roots. Since the mid-1990s,

CALIFORNIA'S NEXT CENTURY 2.0

the percentage of Americans doing this has grown

by over 50%.7 The number of Americans becoming

citizens of other countries has grown seven times in

just the last couple of years.8 However it is difficult

to figure out exactly where Americans are going

and what countries are seeing the most American

immigrants. America is the only industrialized

nation to not keep track of where its people

immigrate to. The US government made an estimate

in 1999, but it was never updated. Roughly it found

that Europe is the major destination, with Germany,

France, Italy, and England twice as popular as any

other European nation. China, Russia, India,

Vietnam, Jamaica, and the Bahamas are the new

major destinations; they have much smaller

amounts of Americans today, but their American

immigration rates are growing much faster than the traditional European destinations.7

The good news is that "American expatriates," when asked about the greatest difficulty living abroad, don't mention anti-Americanism or learning a new language and culture. They cite the tax laws determined by the American government. America is the only major international trading nation that double taxes its citizens. All other major trade nations allow their citizens to be taxed either in the country they moved to or in their origin country, Only America demands that Americans pay taxes in both countries—a situation that is entirely fixable within the confines of America. The American government currently gives so little help or encouragement to Americans living overseas, that the view among expatriates of the American government must be that "the perception is that any American living overseas is there for nefarious reasons." 8

America's Diaspora today, without even trying, is equal to or greater than all of the official government supported Diasporas.

America is still an influential force now—it can improve its global image with the plan provided here and use that improved image and remaining influence to make the emigration of Americans abroad acceptable politically and socially.

American academics have already presented this idea of America strategically reaching out to is Diaspora. David Rothkopf's definition of soft power almost exclusively involves allowing individuals in other nations to accept or reject foreign cultural influences. He also mentions, but only in passing, the use of the English language and consumption of news and popular music and film as cultural dominance that he supports.[7]

---

7 "The American Diaspora," *Esquire*, September 26 2008

8 Giles Broom, "Wealthy Americans queue to give up their passports", *Bloomberg,* May 1, 2012

9 David Rothkopf, "In Praise of Cultural Imperialism?" Foreign Policy, June 22, 1997.

Also, former presidential foreign policy advisor Zbigniew Brzezinski has written an entire book on the same concept that says America currently is a global force because of military and hard power, but it should give up that sort of power in pursuit of equally influencing the world through soft power. This will require a radical shift in American policy and America itself.[8] Also, the government has already investigated this idea; in 2011, the federal government held a conference among top international thinkers called The Future of US Foreign Policy: "The Revival of Soft Power and Cultural Diplomacy?" In 2004, The American Conservative magazine stated that America is missing strategic thinking about how to reach out to

---

10 Zbigniew Brzezinski, *The Choice: Global Domination or Global Leadership* (New York: Basic Books, 2004)

the world, and that is hurting the war on terror.[9]

Even American business people are saying that

Americans need to be better at international

relations in order to stop hurting the American

economy.[10]

Recently, California's state government authored a

report studying how global empires directly impact

California's economy.[11]

America's transition to this new form of empire

will be greatly helped by an independent

---

11 Paul Schroeder, "Misreading the 9/11 Report: Victory in the War on Terror Depends Less on Homeland Security Than Global Collaboration," *American Conservative*, September 13, 2004.

12 James M. Pethokoukis, "America's Image Problem: But Dislike of US Policy May Not Hurt Products," *US News*, September 17, 2006.

13 Anna Lee Saxenian, "Local and Global Networks of Immigrant Professionals in Silicon Valley," PPIC, 2002.

CALIFORNIA'S NEXT CENTURY 2.0

California. Americans are not very aware of foreign nations, even other ones that speak English, such as Australia and England and South Africa. Seeing a former US state become a foreign country and still keeping up on news and information and being in communication with California will ease America's transition into learning and networking with foreign countries. By starting with the newly independent state of California, the average American will become familiar with keeping up on foreign nations and realize it is not that difficult to understand them.

CHAPTER 3: THE WORLD LITERALLY NEEDS A "NEW SWITZERLAND FOR THE NEXT CENTURY"

Story 3: The world literally needs a "New Switzerland for the next century"

SUPERPOWERS OF THE FUTURE WORLD

NOW: 1985–2040

After the fall of Communism in 1985, the entire world realized that capitalism and trade was the only way to run a country. What was previously thought of as the "Western way" or "America's way" became understood around the world as "the only way." Countries who had thought of capitalism as evil, or a way for Europe and America to colonize them, realized that they could become massive economies by opening up their economy to world trade and investment. Mindset ceased to be what made countries excel.

Now the size of a domestic consumer base determines the size of an economy. Countries with a cohesive government and the largest populations become the new and surviving superpowers. The map above shows the main population of these countries where the overwhelming majority of the population lives, a.k.a. the "actual Chinese people or American people," not their national boundaries, which typically are filled with vast uninhabited spaces. Of the six superpowers of the future, only

Europe and India actually populate their entire national boundaries.

TRADE AND CUSTOMS UNIONS OF THE WORLD

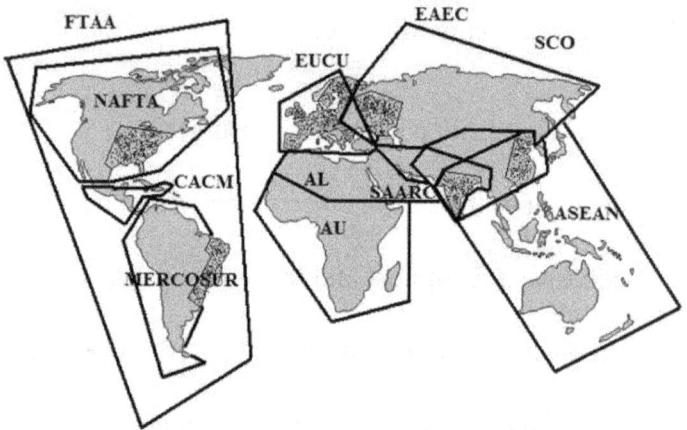

NOW: 1990–2000–2010

The map above is very confusing—it is designed to be, to give an impression of the current level of global political order. Starting after the fall of Communism, many regions of the world developed customs or trade unions with full-member countries

and observation-member countries (the ability to

attend meetings but no voting or speaking rights).

Observation-member countries are those that the

customs union wants to join and is working to have

join, but it will take some time for the political and

economic details to be worked out. As is the main

point of the map above, many of these customs and

trade blocs overlap. This means that different trade

unions, all dominated by one main member (the

superpowers shown above), compete with each

other for attention of dual-member countries

(nations that belong to more than one trade or

customs union).

America dominates the NAFTA, while Brazil

dominates the MERCOSUR, but both nations and

all of the other countries in the entire Western Hemisphere are part of FTAA. Each organization does essentially the same thing: provides economic and social links between countries to bring them closer together. However, since superpowers are gigantically larger than other normal size countries, the trade unions serve the objective of binding smaller countries to the much larger superpower. When trade blocs overlap, this means that superpowers compete with each other for dominance in political and economic negotiations.

The European Union has a customs union, EUCU, which absorbed many of the former countries that were part of the USSR while it was still a functioning governmental organization. However, Russia, still a superpower, has decided that it wants to compete for the attention of the former USSR

states and has created its own customs union. The

EAEC, which competes with Europe for

membership of the same countries that are between

Europe and Russia—mostly former USSR

countries. The large country of Ukraine is a nation

where Russia and Europe are competing against

each other for attention. The former countries of

Czechoslovakia are another set of nations being

competed for.

The Arab League is a union of Middle Eastern

countries and Turkey. However, Turkey is also part

of the European trade bloc. India has a trade bloc

called SAARC, which includes Pakistan and

Afghanistan. However, Russia's EAEC has shown

interest in bringing Afghanistan into its sphere of

influence. Both countries are aware that America is trying to build Afghanistan as a close ally to herself.

Not to be without her own sphere due to quickly rising prominence, China has developed SCO, which includes India, Pakistan, Iran, and Russia— the USSR's former Central Asian countries which are also part of Russia's EAEC. However, Russia, India, and China are all part of ASEAN, a trade bloc focused on the Southeast Asian nations.

THE OLD ORDER

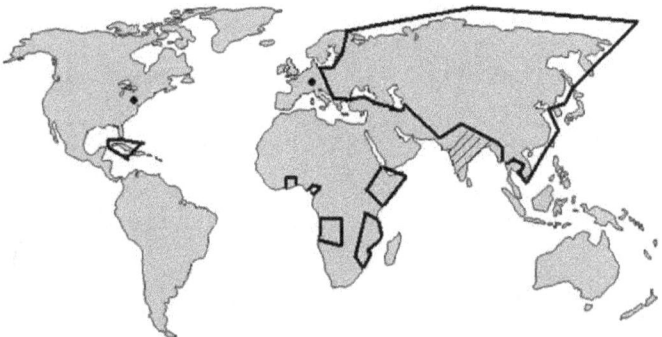

1945–1985–1990

CALIFORNIA'S NEXT CENTURY 2.0

Starting with the end of WWII and continuing for most of this last century, the world had a much simpler order. The world was broken up into just two customs and trade blocs: those that believed in communism both as a political and economic system, and those that believed in capitalism and trade as the economic system and democracy as the political system. All world negotiations of political and economic issues between the two blocs and within the capitalism bloc countries occurred at the UN headquarters in New York in America and in Geneva in Switzerland. Russia was the superpower that was dominant in the communist bloc, and America was the superpower that was dominant in the capitalism bloc. India alone dealt with both the capitalist and communist blocs. Many angry meetings took place in the UN, but while the superpowers and their allies talked, major wars

never broke out.

THE PREVIOUS ORDER

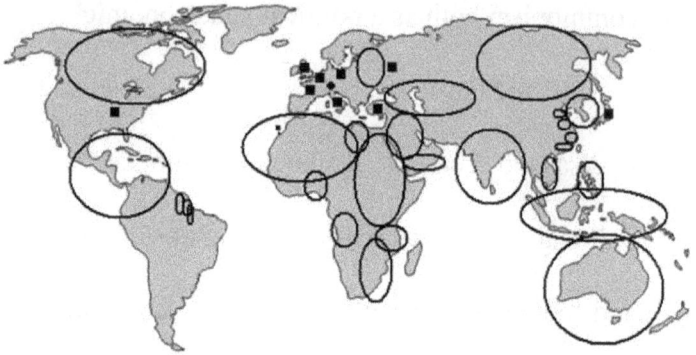

Squares = superpowers

Circles = colonized areas

1815–1908

Before this time, Europe was still finishing

off the Renaissance era that brought it out of the

medieval period. During this epoch, it was

completing its transformation through the Industrial

Revolution, where modern machines were first built and modern governments first appeared. The age of kings was over, and democratic governments based on laws, with respect for business and trade, were formalized. During this era known as the Second Industrial Revolution, the concepts of modern government and industry did not just affect Europe but spread to the rest of the globe. The whole world caught up to these concepts. During this time of mostly European superpowers (England, France, Holland, Germany, Austro-Hungarian Empire, Italy, and Russia), but including America, Japan, and Turkey, all negotiations for political and trade occurred in just Geneva, Switzerland. Though great powers with large armies and the power to move those armies anywhere in the world existed, this was largely a peaceful time, just like the Cold War era discussed above. The possibility for world war was always there, but it never happened; instead only small conflicts in faraway places occurred, and there were only a few of them.

The world powers traded openly among each other; this is why the Second Industrial Revolution is called the First Age of International Trade. The era after the Cold war, when all countries realized they needed to engage in economic capitalism, is not the first time the modern world has seen complete global trade among all nations; it is the second time. All of the powers met and negotiated every aspect and every last-minute detail of trade between their nations and colonies—including finance rates, customs duties, rules for shipping, communications, medicine, scientific sharing, and for war when it did happen—in the city of Geneva, Switzerland.

In this era, every nation that was a superpower spread out to colonize every available piece of land in the world. They mined it for raw materials that could be sold through the colonizing nation to other colonizing nations, who would then sell it to their colony nations. It was not completely open or fair free trade, but the entire world was connected in one massive global trade system where every country contributed materials that they could make. Most manufacturing of raw materials into industrial goods occurred in the colonial nations. This system worked for about one hundred years during which the world underwent many changes in science, technology, transportation and government. The standard of living of the industrial nations increased by gigantic leaps. It was largely a peaceful time in that major wars between industrial nations essentially didn't happen.

The era of 1913 to 1945 would see a time where all of the industrial nations went to war to try to knock the other out and decrease the number of superpowers to just a coalition of a few of the original powers. Every industrial nation tried to figure out what winning combination would place itself in the much smaller group of powers who would rule the world and be able to take over the raw material nations that the fallen nations previously ruled. Japan and Italy are two examples of nations that switched sides during different times in this era, seeking to be on the winning side. While ideology is claimed to be the cause of World Wars I and II, jockeying to be part of the winning coalition and claim more territories is really what this period of global war was about.

The common story told of the start of the world wars is that all of the industrial nations joined competing military agreements to support each other in war and that a government head of one of the nations of one of the military blocs was assassinated. However, the real start of this period of world wars began only a few years prior during 1908–1913. What happened in this extremely small period is that the world order of open, fully international trade ended. The superpowers stopped trading with each other and closed their borders to trade, immigration, finance, and the exchange of ideas. Germany, France, England, America, Japan, Italy, Russia, Turkey, and Austro-Hungary all formed trade walls with other powers and traded among themselves and their colonies in the hopes of preventing other industrial nations from overtaking them in a world of free trade. This short period that ended a system that worked for one hundred years is known as the end of the Second Industrial Revolution. The key piece of this era is that all of the nations stopped talking and negotiating as they had done in Geneva, Switzerland. Japan walking out of the Geneva meeting hall; Germany's refusal to attend meetings and its public violation of agreements made in Geneva; the Soviet Union leaving the organization altogether—all during the year 1939—are only the most famous examples. But from then on, all of the powers took negotiations at Switzerland less seriously, and a

system that had worked for one hundred years

collapsed within five years.

BACK TO TODAY

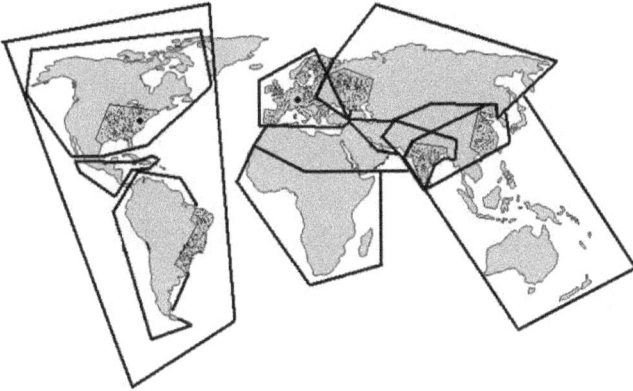

2011–2040–?

Global economists expect all of the new

superpowers will be at full strength by 2040.

Known as the "BRIC countries," Brazil, Russia,

India, and China will join the EU and the USA as the complete set of superpowers until an unknown time (some time past 2040). During this time, the trend has been and will be of increasing global trade at an incredible rate but also a complete breakdown in the old order of discussion of issues amongst nations. The UN and Switzerland used to be the centers for all discussions among all nations and especially the superpowers. Now each established superpower is spending most of their energy developing their own coalition of nations instead of just negotiating through the UN and in Switzerland. All of the new trade and customs unions are a reaction to the fact that the UN has been in America and largely led and directly financed by America. Even Europe, America's closest ally, is not happy that America has dominated the UN for most of the last century. The creation of the EU is a reaction to counterbalance the size of America.

Brussels, the capital of the EU, is used more by European countries as the location for all political and economic discussion than the UN. India and Brazil have complained that they are not on the UN Security Council, the leadership group of the UN, even though they will be superpowers soon. Russia has always thought of the UN as a machine by America and Europe to check its power and growth, and that opinion has not changed since the fall of the USSR. It's important to recognize that although America is the main financer and principal participant in the UN, the average American does not like the UN, wants America out of it, and is openly hostile to its general existence. Fueling this sentiment are scandals: of UN peacekeeping nations organizing mass rape of the people they are protecting and the Oil for Food scandal for Iraq (where many Iraqis needlessly suffered and the UN's ability to undertake an embargo—its main tool for change—was undercut). The reputation of the organization from these scandals was, according to some, impossible to fix. All of the nations, except for America, have publicly discussed leaving the IMF, the international bank that has given all governments in the world loans for most of the last century, because it is dominated by Americans and Europeans. The SCO was started as a direct challenge by Russia and China to the UN. The WTO, the organization that is designed to hold all of the new discussions needed by a growing world economy, routinely shuts down, has meetings that are cancelled, has members who do not show, or ends with no agreements being made. The WTO was designed to handle the extra negotiations that a globalized economy would need that would overburden the existing UN. Now most nations are less interested in the UN and the WTO and are forming their own regional economic blocs where they, the superpower, are the dominant partner, as they see America in these organizations. Most 2011 meetings of the WTO ended in blockades and no agreements in the "Doha round." The organization designed to take some of the pressure off the WTO by focusing only on the major economic nations, the G8 (now the G20), also routinely shuts down or ends meetings with no agreement. Mark Weisbrot of the Center for Economic and Policy Research stated, "I can't think of a time when the US has been more isolated…And that can't help when nations are trying to reach consensus in the WTO."[12]

Echoing this sentiment, Zbigniew Brzezinski, a former foreign policy advisor to a US president says in his book *Strategic Vision: America and the Crisis of Global Power* that America's image in the world has greatly shrunk. According to Brzezinski, this is dangerous because of the fact there are new powers in the world rising and because of the complexity of the new world issues. So many more independent players in the last two decades makes the future very dangerous because without someone trying to

---

[12] Nusrat Choudhury, "The Economic Impact of Anti-Americanism" (working paper, Princeton University, 2005).

pull them all to the negotiating table, these powers are more likely to go their own way on a range of issues, which could lead to military confrontation when two independent nations' "own ways" bump into each other. Since these nations are not talking and there are so many overlaps in the regions that new powers want to have influence, the chance for a future of high military conflict is very probable. Brzezinski's answer is for America to improve her standing in the world's eye so that she can continue to provide this central leadership role. In addition, the world needs America to retain her position of global leadership because otherwise it will result in a world that has lost its will to engage in negotiation and dialogue at a time when world issues need dialogue most.

The difference between that book and this analysis is that Brzezinski assumes: a) America can make radical changes on her own, domestically, that will allow it to grow big again and b) the world would allow and be open to a renewed American leadership in all world affairs, just as it was for the last century. This is in contrast to a view that the world has fundamentally shifted and that nations that are just as wealthy and as large as America wouldn't want America to lead them in a new world order, especially since they had no choice but to watch America lead for nearly the last one hundred years. This analysis argues that Brzezinski is mistaken: people around the world fundamentally don't think that way. Even if America did everything right, the world has changed and now other players can wield as much influence in their sections of the world as America has previously wielded. Simply out of a sense of positive self-identity, not hate against anyone else, major powers of the future will not want anyone to be higher than them in the international order of the future world—or to lead them. And simply being talked to "that way" will only grow the irritation of powers as they shrink the gap between the size of their economies and America's—a gap that will inevitably close, with a world of equals being the result. Some political theorists have speculated that the world may remember the Cold War as the peaceful era compared to this new era being discovered. For example, only one genocide had existed since the end of WWII during the time of the Cold War (Cambodia), but since the fall of Communism and

the end of the Cold War, there have been six
(Rwanda, Sri Lanka, Sudan, Bosnia, Burma, East
Timor). It is yet to be seen, but so far, there is
reason to believe that this new era might be seen as
the era of instability and war compared to the time
of the Cold War. Return to the era of 1908 to 1913.
The world was full of international trade for a
century but then broke into separate regional trade
blocs, and concurrently stopped talking at the
agreed upon international negotiating nexus of
Geneva, Switzerland. Then came world war. Today,
the world started off with increasing international
trade from 1985, but within ten to fifteen years, by
2000, the world had developed into trade customs
unions dominated by a separate current or future
superpower. Concurrently, separate negotiation
centers and conferences were developed by each

superpower that competed equally for their attention with the UN. The similarities, while not exact, are extremely similar in pattern. Will the world return to an era where superpowers attempt to form coalitions to knock each other out and the entire planet erupts into decades of conflict that reach to every country until there is a final winner—after atrocities and destruction on levels the world has never known before—even with its horrible past of incredible warfare? Russia and America almost went to war during the war in Bosnia in the late 1990s. Russian troops almost fought American troops during the recent war in Georgia. American politicians routinely talk about going to war with China. China has in the last couple of years warned India that the entire Southeast Asian ocean belongs to them, alone, and not anyone else, not even the

Southeast Asian nations. India has talked about a Chinese plan called a "ring of pearls" designed to encircle them with naval bases. America has tried to open up Burma, a country next to India that has been under Chinese sponsorship for the last fifty years. Europe is pursuing a direct economic link to Latin America, traditionally America's economic backyard. And all of the traditional international organizations for discussions are having less productive meetings, while new, more regional negotiation centers open up. Perhaps nothing will happen. Or perhaps, the world won't drag closer to an era where the ground has been set for an easy opening to WWIII. Perhaps the world will simply not integrate economically as much as it could, many nations will never grow economically, and billions (the majority of the earth's population) will remain mired in poverty. International trade will stop and level, industrial nations with the right mentality about world trade will only grow a little bit more, and then wages will never rise again for anyone. Every economy will stagnate as countries trade and partner with each other less. Scientific inventions that would have been made by a cooperation of resources, as exploded during the Second Industrial Revolution, won't happen. And scientific discovery and the improvement of living standards too will plateau for everyone. Wars in different parts of the world, while small, will continue on for decades instead of being negotiated within a few years, sparing millions of lives. Instead, pockets of the world will just be known as permanent war zones, similar to what happened in Mexico and Colombia during the early 1900s.

CALIFORNIA'S NEXT CENTURY 2.0

So much could be lost with the loss of a world talk and negotiation nexus and, equally powerful, so much could fail to be gained.

THE WORLD NEEDS A NEW SWITZERLAND FOR THE NEXT CENTURY

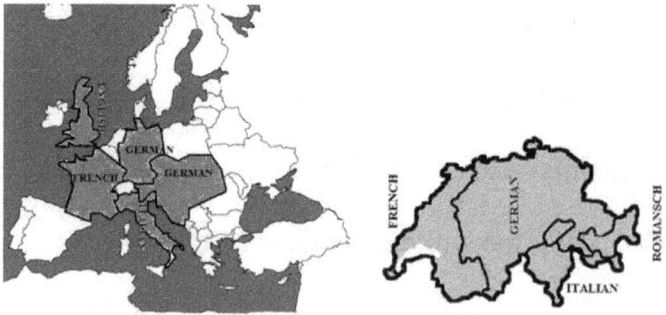

1800s to 1900s

When Europe was at the height of world power, during the Second Industrial Revolution, roughly the century between 1800 and 1900, Switzerland was the negotiation center for the modern world.

Consider:

- The first agreement on international shipping

- The first agreement on international telegraph communications

- The first international intellectual property rules

- The first rules of warfare (the Geneva conventions)

- The main school for international ship captains

- The first international humanitarian organization (the Red Cross)

- The first world health organization (WHO)

- The headquarters of the World Trade Organization (and the organization that governed world trade before it, the GATT)

- The location of the first degree in international relations at the Geneva school of diplomacy and international relations

- And almost every other significant business, political, medical, and scientific international agreement in the world

These were all debated, talked about, and agreed upon in Geneva, Switzerland.

From 1800 to 1900, and even during the "inter-world war eras," the world superpowers met at Geneva, Switzerland. The first attempt to provide rules of war was in Geneva in 1864, in the Geneva conventions. This was also the first attempt at establishing what is now known as "international law" in general. Besides being the other major office of the UN for world negotiations on everything, Geneva was also the site of the first attempt at a UN in 1892, the Inter-Parliamentary Union. It was the site of the second attempt at a UN in 1920, where the first full meeting of the "League of Nations" was held. And it was the site of the closest the modern world has ever come to an end to war, the "World Disarmament Conference" held in 1932 (one year before Japan left the League of Nations in Geneva and Germany violated all treaties it had signed in that city). After WWII, although more activity would move to the UN at New York City, much of the negotiations between the two new world poles still occurred at Geneva. The Geneva

Summit of 1955, between all of the winners of

WWII, established the boundaries of the Cold War

powers' spheres. The end of the Cold War also was

started in Geneva, in 1985, in the Second Geneva

Summit, where the president of America and the

leader of the Soviet Union met for the first time and

discussed "Glasnost," or the opening up the Soviet

economy, which led to the eventual downfall of the

Soviet Union. People familiar with Switzerland

would say this is because of: their hard policy on

nonintervention in any other nation's policies; their

position as the world's bankers, holding monies for

all of the nations of Europe, and being able to

exchange each nation's moneys between the

nations; being held in high respect for their

technical achievements during this century; being

the world's premier location for the development of

watches (one of the most complicated, frequently used machines during that era); and their cultural and globally unique tendency to inherently seek for collaborative decision making from small to large decisions. Also, during this era, Switzerland was known as the retreat for the wealthy, with its breathtaking views of the mountains, the clean air (while the rest of Europe was covered in smog from industrial machines), and skiing—a popular pastime for the wealthy who could afford hobbies and vacations. While these are the reasons that Europe saw Switzerland as a natural fit for the European-dominated world order, it is the not reason why these conditions existed in Switzerland. Switzerland became Europe's money holders, money changers, and watch makers (which led it to be its negotiation center) because of an earlier condition: it was a

European nation, the *only* European nation, made up of most of the different peoples of Europe. Switzerland lived the example of Europe working together; it did not just popularize the idea. Since the medieval ages, Switzerland had been one nation made up of Italian, French, German, and Romansch (similar to Romanian) peoples. It spoke all of these languages. It was the only independent nation in Europe that was composed of many types of Europeans. Other European countries had minorities that spoke another language, but they were treated as outcasts instead of equal partners in the nation. Respect for diversity as a strength essentially only existed in Switzerland from the 1500s to the 1950s. In the early 1800s, in order to encourage more banking business from the rising empire of England, it instituted a national English language education program and added English as the fifth major language that most Swiss people could comfortably use (the average Swiss person speaks three languages). France and Italy were major powers, as were Germany and the Austro-Hungarian empire which also spoke a Germanic language. English was spoken in Switzerland, which allowed America to easily be reached out to. This left only Turkish, Russian, and Japanese as languages of superpowers not spoken by the average Swiss person. While most of the power negotiations of the world from 1800 to 1900, through the world wars, and after them from 1950 to 1985, occurred in Geneva, this "post-Cold War" or "Multi-Polar Order" is different. As explained above, most of the new powers, and some of the old, are trying to leave the traditional sources of negotiation and make their own competing sources of negotiation for everything (trade, politics, security, environment, etc). The situation has become so energized that even Geneva is beginning to question its worth as a global negotiation center. **In 2011, the mayor of Geneva publicly called for a debate on whether Geneva, and the UN in general, were still working as their historical roles in the world.**[13] And the Swiss government sponsored a formal report examining if the IMF was still worthwhile in the new world order.[14]

---

[13] Jean-Christophe Nothias, "Talk of Geneva: Geneva and Its Global Role," *The Global Journal,* January 19. 2011.

[14] Jose De Gregorio, Barry Eichengreen, Takatoshi Ito, and Charles Wyplosz, "An Independent and Accountable IMF: Geneva Report on the World Economy." *Center for Economic Policy Research,* http://www.cepr.org/press/geneva_report.htm

CALIFORNIA'S NEXT CENTURY 2.0

<u>The Facts and Fictions of Global Acceptance</u>

The global situation is even more dangerous when the fact that, contrary to popular news, the world is becoming less tolerant of diversity as it becomes increasingly technologically connected, not more tolerant. While the world is pulling away from the traditional negotiation and communication areas, most nations are also becoming steadily less tolerant of people who are not from their country in general. Furthermore, also contrary to popular opinion, technology has not significantly decreased the sense of distance between places and therefore peoples. Most people around the world use technology to stay more connected within their country, not connected to foreign nations, again despite popular opinion. Technology so far shows no signs of making the world significantly more connected than it was in the past. This combined dynamic makes a strong suggestion that a skilled negotiation center that can bring people together from different nations is a resource that the future of the world will still need for a long time.

The World Is Not Diverse

Several experts agree that most of the Western world is actually xenophobic to foreigners and internal minorities. Worse yet, those in the West won't admit they have a problem, so they are nowhere near being able to fix the issue.[15] Australia, along with England, France, Denmark, Holland, and Canada, began massive immigration of peoples

---

[15] Jonathan Cush and Sujata Ramachandran, "Xenophobia, International Migration and Human Development," The UN Development Programme, 2009; Simon Toubeau, "Social Democracy and Regional Nationalism in Multi-Level Systems," Oxford, 2010; Dr. Anwen Elias, "Whither a Europe of the Regions: Minority Nationalist Parties and the Challenges of European Integration," University of Wales, 2007.

from different cultures, from very different parts of
the earth, roughly in the late 1970s and early 1980s.
France and Denmark recently had mass minority
riots, Holland for the first time ever has a nativist
party whose platform is no more immigrants, and
English racism against Indian peoples is well-
known and well established in that country. In 2005
Australia had a riot against all Lebanese and WOG
people. And none of these countries has achieved
anything over 10% of their population being of a
minority descent. Traditionally diverse nations such
as India, Brazil, Mexico, Kazakhstan, Ukraine,
Thailand, Malaysia, and Myanmar are all full of
institutionalized ethnic discrimination and mass
poverty. Very few historically diverse nations have
actual positive relations among all of their groups
and a standard of civil rights for all.

Pulling Away from Talk Nexus

The US National Intelligence Council notes, "Emerging powers show ambivalence toward global institutions…like the UN and IMF…Traditional alliances will weaken…This is a story with no clear outcome…[and is] without precedent in modern history."[16] In "The Future of World Trade," Alexander Neubacher notes, "After WTO negotiations failed last week, experts worry whether the Doha talks will be continued at all."

Many experts make the same conclusion in a variety of media outlets including *Time*, CNN, *New York Times Magazine*, and *American Political Science*

---

[16] *Global Trends 2025: A Transformed World*, (US National Intelligence Council, 2008).

CALIFORNIA'S NEXT CENTURY 2.0

Review.[17] *Global Paradox*, by John Naisbitt, stated

it bluntly, "First of all the G-7 summit is a relic of

---

[17] Renato Ruggiero, "The Future of the World Trading System, Address to the Institute for International Economics Conference, Washington DC," WTO News 1998; Fareed Zakaria, "The Rise of the Rest," *Time* 2008; Dani Rodrik, "Leaderless Global Governance," Straights Times, 2012; Richard Quest, "Welcome to 'Davos Do Little,'" CNN, 2012; Parag Khanna, "Waving Goodbye to Hegemony," *New York Times Magazine*, 2008; Mohamed A El-Erain, "Bank Shot: The Eurozone's Banking Crisis Is on the Verge of Becoming a Global Economic Catastrophe. But Do the Economic Heavyweights Meeting in Washington This Week Know What to Do About It?" Foreign Policy, 2011; James Traub, "Wallowing in Decline," 2010; "The United Nations & Global Intervention," Cato Policy Report, 1997; Michael Barone, "Losing the Stomach for Humanitarian Interventions," 2010; John O'Sullivan, "Days of Our Globe: A Geopolitical Soap Opera," 2002; Joshua Muravchik, "The Future of The United Nations Understanding the Past to Chart a Way Forward," American Enterprise Institute; "Rethinking Global Institutions: Do We Have the International Tools to Fight the Global Economic Crisis?" American Enterprise Institute, 2009; David Held and Anthony McGrew, eds. "Governing Globalization: Power, Authority and Global Governance," *American Political Science Review*, 2002, 37, 41, 84, 204; Samuel Huntington, "The Clash of Civilizations: The Remaking of the World Order," 1996, 194, 209, 306, 307, 317, 321; Phillip Bobbitt, *The Shield Of Achilles: War, Peace, and the Course of History* (2002), 716.

the Cold War and the energy crisis of the 1970s.

Second, the kind of leadership that was appropriate

during the Cold War and before the great revolution

in telecommunications is obsolete." Dutch

sociologist Saskia Sassen points out that the world

needs more discussion because it is becoming more

complex and more nations are growing in the

international field. Ironically, just the opposite is

occurring in participating international

institutions.[18] The situation of the world pulling

away from traditional negotiation centers is also

pushed by America. Americans increasingly don't

trust the foreign world or even international

institutions, regardless of the fact that it made them,

and they are increasingly ideologically pulling out

---

[18] Saskia Sassen, *Globalization and Its Discontents* (The New Press, 1998), 197, 199, 200, 214.

of them.[19] For many academics this behavior pattern of the current era reminds them too much of the dangerous period that led to WWI.[20] In *Shield of Achilles*, Phillip Bobbitt theorizes that the world could turn into what he calls the "the Garden" where large markets disconnect from each other and form regional trading blocs that do not interact with each other and are hostile to each other.

---

[19] Virginia Postrel, *The Future and Its Enemies: The Growing Conflict Over Creativity, Enterprise, and Progress* (Simon and Schuster, 1998), 2–3, 204; David Held and Anthony McGrew, eds., "Governing Globalization: Power, Authority and Global Governance" *American Political Science Review*, 2002, 38, 242–243.

[20] Bartosz Stanislawski, "A More Secure World? In Some Ways Yes; In Some Ways No," Cato Institute, 2011; Martin Sieff, "That 1914 Feeling: The Lights Are Going Out, Again," *The American Conservative*, 2003; Robert Locke, "Nation Busting: The Trouble with Globalism," *The American Conservative*, 2003; Richard Watson, "Future Files: The 5 Trends That Will Shape the Next 50 Years," 2008, 69.

And just because more of the World's nations are becoming democracies doesn't mean that there will be any more talking or coordination in the future, than if most of the World's nations stayed dictatorships. As pointed out by the *New York Times* writer Charles A Kupchan, in 2012, in a article entitled "America's Place in the New World"; "And just because more countries are becoming democracies doesn't mean that there will naturally be more consensus." Many democracies don't hold "western values" and still enjoy disagreeing with America for the sake of being seen disagreeing. For example, "Standing up to America still holds cachet in India and Brazil, one reason New Delhi and Brazilia line up with Washington less than 25 percent of the time at the United Nations." The conclusion is that, "This century, in contrast, will be the first time in history in which multiple versions of order and modernity co-exist in an interconnected world; no longer will the West anchor globalization. Multiple power centers, and the competing models they represent, will vie on a more level playing field."

Why is the world turning away from global traditional negotiation and talk centers? For the same reason that it is becoming less tolerant to diversity, or what John Naisbitt termed the "Global paradox."[21] When people are confronted with massive change, more interactions with the whole world, they develop a longing for "the old

---

[21] Also mentioned in "Future Files: The 5 Trends That Will Shape the Next 50 Years," by Richard Watson (2008, pgs. 15, 22, 34, 69, 70), and is the subject throughout the book, *The Invention of Tradition* by Eric Hobsbawm and Terence Ranger (1992).

traditions" as a way of balancing a continued self-identity in the face of so many new identities. Many of England's "traditions" that are practiced today were invented during the turn of the century when London was the most globally connected it had ever been—not the least. Naisbitt says that the same effect is happening today, except for the entire world. As more international information and ideas press upon people, they more they will turn away from them and toward things they regard as "traditional" or "unique" to their country in order to maintain a personal sense of identity.

As shown below, the impulse to pull away when allowed so much connection not only applies to politics but to business, proving the strength of this dynamic, that even when massive amounts of money are at stake, people will still retreat away from international outreach.

Technology has not decreased distance between places, and therefore people. The Internet has not primarily brought people around the world closer together than in the past. The *Internet is mostly used by people to communicate with people who they see in their local towns*. People like interacting with people they can see. And even if the Internet and computers do develop a level of technology that really makes people feel like they're meeting each other in person, there is a limit, it appears, to how much technology and improved non-natural communication that people can take.

"The Internet is primarily a place where people go to find…other like minded individuals," according to Richard Watson.[22] Typically that means their neighbors or other people who live in their local areas.[23]

Furthermore it is not just a preference for purely social interactions; businesses still act like distance matters and prefer to do business locally. Global corporations, although having a worldwide collective presence, primarily do business through a serious of hubs in different nations who only primarily do business with people

---

[22] Richard Watson, "Future files: The 5 Trends That Will Shape the Next 50 Years," 2008, 110.

[23] Terry Heaton, "TV News in a Postmodern World, The Local Web"; Jacob Goldenberg and Moshe Levy, *Distance Is Not Dead: Social Interaction and Geographical Distances in the Internet Era*, The Hebrew University, Israel, 2009.

in that local area; they do not do business with other

businesses located in other countries, or with

anyone who is not located nearby.[24] And all

businesses in general tend to do business with

people they know and physically meet, even over

the Internet.[25]

---

[24] Mohanbir Swahney and Satish Nambisan, *The Global Brain* (Wharton School Publishing, 2008), 231; Erran Carmel and Pamela Abbott, "Why 'Nearshore" Means That Distance Still Matters," 2007); E. Leamer, "A Flat World, a Level Playing Field, a Small World After All, or None of the Above?" *Journal of Economic Literature* 45 (2007): 83–126; Ivan Kandilov and Thomas Grennes, "The Determinants of Service Off Shoring: Does Distance Matter" (2007); A. Disdier and K. Head, "The Puzzling Persistence of the Distance Effect on Bilateral Trade," 2007; F. Kimura Lee, *The Gravity Equation in International Trade in Services* (2006), 92–121; E. Stein and C. Daude, "Longitude Matters: Time Zones and the Location of Foreign Direct Investment," 2007; Paul Krugman, "The Role of Geography in Development," 1998; Jeffrey Frankel, Ernesto Stein, and Shang-Jin Wei, "Chapter 4: The Gravity Model of Bilateral Trade" in *Regional Trading Blocs in the World Economic System* (1997).

[25] B. Blum and A. Goldfarb, "Does the Internet Defy the Law of Gravity?" *Journal of International Economics* 70, (2006): 384–405; Edward Leamer and Michael Storper, "The

CALIFORNIA'S NEXT CENTURY 2.0

Pankaj Ghemawat (in "The Hard Reality of Semiglobalization: And how to profit from it") has shown a global 10% rule, where the world in the age claimed to be the international communications revolution is only 10% internationally connected. Even the most international nations only have about 10% of their phone calls go to international places, only 10% of their college students are foreigners, only 10% of their businesses are interested in international trade, only 10% of their money goes to help another foreign country, only 10% of their money is invested in other economies, only 10% of their economy is made up of foreign money, and

---

Economic Geography of the Internet Age," 2001; Keith Head, Thierry Mayer, and John Ries, "Service Offshoring: Same Old Trade With a New Label?" 2007; Tim Harford, "How Email Brings You Closer to the Guy in the Next Cubicle," 2008; Mario Polèse, "Is Distance Really Dead? Comparing Industrial Location Patterns over Time in Canada," 2004.

only 10% of their tourists are foreigners. He holds his proof that the world is not that much more global, as he followed this trend for over a decade and it still remained at 10% despite all the global media constantly reporting a rise in international relations. Other studies support this conclusion.[26]

Even the largest military in the world with the largest global presence still recognizes that "distance in military affairs" matters in all activities.[27]

---

[26] Laura Crossett, "The World Is Not Flat," 2005; Aqueil Ahmad, "The World Is (Not) Flat," 2007.

[27] Kieran Webb, "The Continued Importance of Geographic Distance and Boulding's Loss of Strength Gradient," *Comparative Strategy* 26, no. 4 (2007): 295–310.

"Techno-stress" is a new concept that may mean that even if there were a new super form of technology never before thought of that allowed perfect human connection, there is evidence that new communications technology, said to connect the world, may actually have a limit. This limit may include up to 40% of the population of any area, even advanced nations, not being up for it; women may not enjoy the benefits of technology as much as men. Given that more women are entering the global labor force than ever before, the computer's help in connecting people may reach a definitive plateau—hence the world will increase easy communication because of computers up to a point. There is a limit to how much connection technology can bring.[28]

---

[28] Michele Weil and Larry Rosen, "Technostress," 2007; J.

CALIFORNIA'S NEXT CENTURY 2.0

Besides the promises of the Internet, transportation around the world has not much improved in the modern era either. In 2005, the US Department of Energy released the "Hirsch Report," which said that the world had hit "peak oil" and the global supply of oil, even if new discoveries were made, would only dramatically decrease in the future because of the continued population and economic growth. Currently, all

---

Hollan and S. Stornetta, "Beyond Being There," Proceedings of CHI 92 (1992): 119–125; Natalie Zee, "New Technologies in the Workplace: Approaching the Virtual Office"; Nancy Ramsey and Pamela McCorduck, "Where Are the Women in Information Technology? Preliminary Report of Literature Search and Interviews," 2005; John Todman and Kenneth Day, "Computer Anxiety: The Role of Psychological Gender," 2004; Lisa A. Ennis, "The Evolution of Technostress: Much of What I Found Out About Technostress and Librarians Remains Just as Pertinent Today as It Was 10 Years Ago," 2005; Catherine Durnell Cramton, "The Mutual Knowledge Problem and Its Consequences for Dispersed Collaboration"; Nora Ephron, "And By the Way, the World Is Not Flat," 2006.

transportation by all forms—sea, air, road, train—run on gasoline with no form of transportation having its own independent renewable source. Fast trains that are becoming more popular only go as fast as airplanes, and airplanes appear to have hit their top speed technologically (the Lear jet, a super-fast jet released in the 1980s, has mostly been banned around the world for noise and other pollution). Flying cars do exist, but they are one million dollars each, when the average new car is twenty thousand, and there is no legal system to allow them to travel around freely. Cars, while using less fuel today, still only travel at about the same speed as fifty years ago. Super-fast ships are being developed, but they too will only go as fast as the bullet train and the average plane and will require massive amounts of oil. Furthermore, ocean ships and trains, while growing larger, have not

improved their technology or speed in over sixty

years.[29]

Jeff Rubin and Benjamin Tal from CIBC World

Markets wrote, "Globalization is reversible. Higher

energy prices are impacting transport costs at an

unprecedented rate. So much so that the cost of

moving goods, not the cost of tariffs, is the largest

barrier to global trade today...The explosion in

---

[29] "Researchers Working on Alternative Jet Fuel: Widespread Use Could Be Years or Even Decades Away, Experts Say," Associated Press, 2006; James Harrigan, "Airplanes and Comparative Advantage," 2005; Professor Frankel, "Technological Changes, Transportation Sector/MP-1566," Economic Research Service/USDA; James Anderson and Eric van Wincoop, "Trade Costs," 2004.

global transport costs has effectively offset all of the trade liberalization of the last three decades."[30]

---

[30] Niranjan Rajadhyaksha, "The Rebirth of Distance," 2008.

CHAPTER 4: SWITZERLAND IS NOT DIVERSE FOR THIS WORLD "LIKE IT WAS"

Now–2040

Currently, and in the next couple of decades, the superpowers will be American/European as one identity, and Russian, Indian, Chinese, and Brazilian. Switzerland, being composed of solely European cultures, no longer has the appeal as the global center for the new world's order like it did during the last century. Rather, if there is to be a talk and negotiation nexus for the upcoming century that can achieve the same dynamic as Switzerland

was able to provide to Europe when most of the

world's powers were European, that new nation will

have to be Russian, Indian, Chinese, American,

European, and Brazilian. It will have to have these

peoples, or most of them having lived together for a

long time, long enough that it is now permanently

part of that nation's culture to be this particular mix

of nations, and, or in combination, it will have to

have the languages and cultures of those nations

spoken and adopted lovingly by the average citizen.

As strange as it sounds, there are a few places in the

world that meet this exceptionally unique

demographic mix.

CALIFORNIA'S NEXT CENTURY 2.0

GLOBAL CONTENDERS FOR "NEW SWITZERLAND FOR THE NEXT CENTURY"

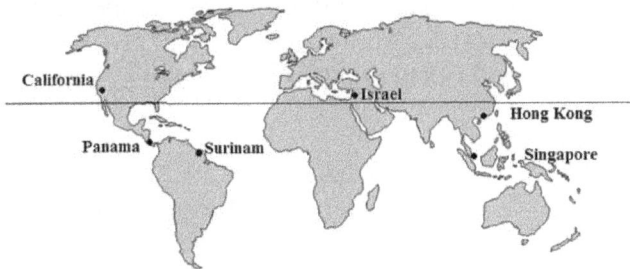

Now

Through unique histories, about six areas on the planet, of over two hundred current nations, have achieved a level of diversity of their domestic populations that resembles all the new superpowers in anything close to the dynamic that Switzerland had over Europe during the Second Industrial Revolution. Of the six, four are not American states:

- Panama has been an American colony for nearly a century and recently has added a substantial Chinese population. It speaks Spanish, one the main European languages, and is a place well-known to Europeans and the world because of its location as a trade gateway.

- Surinam has been a nation of Chinese and Indian immigrant laborers who came in the 1800s; plus it speaks Dutch, a European language from its time as a colony, and has a substantial Brazilian population because of its proximity to Brazil.

- Israel is a contender because of the diverse nations that the Jewish Diaspora traveled to during their time without a nation. It now has substantial populations of Russians and

Europeans, and, because of the close relationship with America since the 1950s, a substantial amount of Americans.

- Hong Kong and Singapore are in the running because of their strong English cultural history resulting from being British trading posts. They also have substantial Chinese and Indian populations who were brought in as immigrant laborers.

In America, two places that are incredibly diverse: the state of California (fourth largest state in America) and the borough of Manhattan Island, a subsection of the city of New York with an area only two-thirds the size of just San Francisco city proper. This is where the similarities end; for diversity in New York City is done entirely differently than diversity in California. New York has almost every nation on the planet represented in this small stretch of land, but they all live in separate ghettos, small block areas where they keep to themselves. One hundred and fifty years after Irish and Italians moved in waves to America, there are still only Irish and only Italian areas in New York where no one outside of these ethnic groups really lives. Additionally, the dominant ethnic group is Anglo-Saxon ("white") with all other ethnicities holding side places in the city's mindset. The most popular American television show set in New York City, *Friends*, had no non-Caucasian significant character until its last season. The second most popular television show set in the same city,

Seinfeld, had none until halfway through its time, and then it only had one.

California, in comparison, is 40% Latino, equal to the Anglo-descent population in most of the state. The most popular television show set in California, *CHiPs*, was based on Latino and Anglo California highway patrol partners. Desegregation of schools happened twenty years earlier in California than in the rest of America, and removal of bans on interethnic marriages occurred thirty years before the same bans in the rest of America. While Manhattan Island in New York City has all of the groups of the world, it does not have them in any significant concentration where they are "the people." Rather, it has small amounts of all of the groups, resembling a living UN. Author Dale

Maharidge said it best: "At their company, Eileen said they have a mix of different ethnicities among their eighteen workers: Black, Chinese, Filipino, Iranian, Latino, Vietnamese, and White. Eileen said there is no ethnic tension. 'Where else in the whole world can you go where you have so many different kinds of people?' Eileen asked of California."[1]

California, since the late 1800s, has had significant populations of not just Europeans (who immigrated directly to California, bypassing the rest of America) and Americans but also Chinese, Indians, and Russians. The only superpower not represented by over a century of significant population presence is Brazilian. However, this is not completely the

---

[1] Dale Maharidge, *The Coming White Minority: California's Eruption and the Nation's Future* (Crown: 1996), 286.

CALIFORNIA'S NEXT CENTURY 2.0

case—reaching out to Brazil, the California Senate

has already commissioned a report on how to link

California and Brazilian cultures by focusing on

existing common characteristics.[2] California signed

a formal agreement with Sao Paolo in Brazil to

jointly develop technology to study the effects of

climate change in 2005. Furthermore, a strong

Brazilian community already exists in Los Angeles,

creating an existing platform for the landing of

many more immigrants, rather than introducing to

California a brand new culture.

---

[2] Senator John Vasconcellos and Assemblyman Tim Leslie, "Toward a California-Brazil Partnership: A Strategic Action Plan," 2004. http://www.docstoc.com/docs/44576441/Brazil-and-California-a-Partnership

Ranking of candidates meeting necessary criteria to become the new Switzerland:

California 5/6

Surinam 4/6

Israel 3/6

Hong Kong 3/6

Singapore 3/6

Panama 3/6

But ethnic connection was not the only thing that made Switzerland "work" as the nexus for Europe. It was a tourist destination: Europeans routinely spent their extra money and time just to be where they loved the scenery and weather.

Singapore, Panama, Hong Kong, and Surinam are all in the equatorial zone, making them hot and humid for most of the year, with a higher than average amount of bugs and disease. This leaves Israel and California as countries with moderate climates.

The Case for California: Tourism

California is the premier world tourism and vacation destination. The California wine country is world famous and Los Angeles is the most traveled-to metro area in the world. San Francisco was selected as the original location of the UN after WWII, and is routinely posted as a selection site for the next world Olympics, while Los Angeles has already hosted the Olympics twice. The California surfer culture of laid-back, sunny days is known throughout the entire world to those with money and time to travel.

Israel, while a world-known traveling destination for religious tourists, also has had trouble the last

three decades with attracting tourism. The biggest
factor is the conflicts caused through its occupation
of Palestinian land and it declaring unilateral
statehood. The last consideration for Switzerland
was its existing presence as a global economic
center, for banking and commerce and the
production of high-value goods. Singapore and
Hong Kong have international reputations as strong
business countries. Singapore is known for its
international trade services, and Hong Kong for its
international banking services. Israel has a strong
economy well-known for research innovation and
Internet technology. While Panama is an
international trade gateway, its economy has always
suffered, and Surinam is considered a poor nation.
Each nation, like Switzerland, is at the crossroads of
different cultural economic regions who have to

pass through this region to trade with each other—
another key point of Switzerland's success. While
the top economic nations listed above are strong,
around the thirtieth ranking in international
economics, California has routinely held the world
position for fifth largest economy, only dropping to
eighth. No other contender nation has achieved a
position relatively close even to California's
weakened economic rating, placing California
above most of the economically strong independent
nations already. Furthermore, California is globally
known for research and innovation (the Internet was
invented here, as was the personal computer and
international jet travel), high education (half of
America's top universities are in California alone),
international finance (San Francisco Market Street),
and international fashion (garment district, Los

Angeles). Regarding international trade, the Port of Long Beach and Los Angeles is the world's second largest trade port. LAX is the world's third largest air trade port. Few large nations come even close to the economic presence that California has had for the last four decades, and none of the other contender nations comes within anything even relatively near to its resources. The given considerations for Switzerland are that it is seen as fair and accountable, has a "well-running" government, and that it is viewed as independent.

California, for all of the news of its troubled government, is one of the best candidates for the responsibility that will be required to act this role. California has an extremely responsive democratic system. Noted as individualist, it leads the nation in initiatives where the public designs the whole bill directly, bringing actual legislation the closest to direct democracy. "The most famous ballot initiative [direct democracy initiative] was prop 13 in 1978 in California."[3] Others contend that "California may be the best example of a state that had such a progressive reaction against machines. The state was hostile toward parties, lacked any type of patronage system, and held nonpartisan elections. Precinct and ward elections were weak, while individual candidates were assertive. Party organizations were once banned from endorsing candidates in primary contests...California was the exception to the rule. Throughout the 1800s, most states

---

[3] Kevin Smith, Alan Greenblatt, John Buntin, and Charles Clark, *Governing States and Localities* (CQ Press College, 2005), pg 121

essentially treated parties as private associations and chose not to regulate them."[4]

A national study by Columbia University reviewed the match between what the public wants and the laws that states pass and found that California was number one in a direct link of delivering legislation that meets the public's needs.[5]

Another academic review found that California is perhaps the best example in all of America for strong direct democracy:

---

[4] Ibid pg 140.

[5] Megan Burke and Maureen Cavanaugh, "Book Explores Fixes for California's Broken Government," *KPBS,* August 3, 2010.

CALIFORNIA'S NEXT CENTURY 2.0

- California is one of seven states that have every possible avenue of direct democracy available to the citizenry.

- California is one of four states with over 251 amendments to its state constitution. The majority of states of America make less than 150 in their entire history.

The authors concluded, "In California, a state with a long, policy-specific constitution that provides for a high degree of direct democracy, they often attempt to amend the constitution instead. While the majority of political scientists wring their hands about this tendency, it undeniably gives Californians a role in shaping

their constitutions that voters in regions of the
country like New England lack."[6]

Sinking in this truth is that the recall of Governor
Davis, which led to the election of Governor
Schwarzenegger, although not as formal and
dignified as traditional elections, was an example
of direct democracy that no other state in
America has. No governor has ever been recalled
since 1921.[7]

---

[6] Kevin Smith, Alan Greenblatt, John Buntin, and Charles
Clark, *Governing States and Localities* (CQ Press College
2005), 73, 83, 123.

[7] "Initiative, Referendum, and Recall: 'Direct Democracy,'"
Extremeprep.org, accessed May 3, 2012,
http://extempprep.org/directdemocracy.html; "Power to the
People: The California Recall and Direct Democracy," Hoover
Institution, July 30, 2003.

CALIFORNIA'S NEXT CENTURY 2.0

The California government is also one of the most professional and efficient in all of America, far beyond neighboring American states: California has the least bureaucracy per capita of any state in America; "California legislature is one of the best equipped and most professional in the country"; and California has a lower number of total legislators than two-thirds of the states in America.[8]

---

[8] Kevin Smith, Alan Greenblatt, John Buntin, and Charles Clark, *Governing States and Localities* (CQ Press College, 2005), 187, 205, 309.

CALIFORNIA'S NEXT CENTURY 2.0

California does have the ability to rationally do money—known by the Federal government. The Public Pension Coordinating Council of the National Association of State Retirement Administrators has also ranked public retirement system management and administration across the country since 2002: thirty-one states make the list—almost half of the states aren't even mentioned for any sort of excellence. Of these, only eleven states are mentioned more than once. Of these, only Texas and Missouri match California for the number of mentions. Of the six times that Money Management Letter has given out awards for excellence in investment for governments, California won in 2005, 2006, and 2007.

And despite all of the debate, and diversity of people and opinion, an academic review found that California has more internal unity than three-fifth of all other states in America.[9]

Sub-national sovereignty for California will be enough to convince the world of independence from America, and therefore deserving of world trust as an independent, fair platform for global discussion, because of a few factors. First is that *California already has a well-established culture independent from America that is viewed as such by the world. California is already known by the Superpowers.*

---

[9] Daniel Elazar, *American Federalism: A View from the States* (Harper Collins College Division, 1972), 16–17.

CALIFORNIA'S NEXT CENTURY 2.0

Russia: President Medvedev came to California in 2010 to talk about how Russia specifically admired California's innovation spirit (the Russian president had previously met the California governor personally). In 2009 Russia's foreign minister said Russia would help support maintenance of Fort Ross in California because of its Russian history. In 2007 Russia's foreign minister said Russia would recognize independent California in comparison to America's recognition of Kosovo.

China: In 2011 the gigantic Bay Bridge was contracted to China to build. Only years earlier China asked the California-created Google company to set up Internet for the entire nation. The globally recognized Google company was started by recent Chinese and Russian immigrants to

CALIFORNIA'S NEXT CENTURY 2.0

California, a fact noted with great pride in both giant countries. Recently China asked another California company, CA Technologies, to develop cloud computing in China. And recently because of the good work on the Bay Bridge, California asked China to bid on construction of the super-gigantic high-speed rail project. Recently, Governor Schwarzenegger traveled to China to make trade deals between that nation and California specifically.

The links are far beyond commercial. Yao Ming, China's most famous athlete, has created a business to bring California wine to China because he knows that California "means luxury" to Chinese. Recently Chinese visitors were the largest foreign travelers to California from any nation. Of all of the Chinese who traveled to America, 50% traveled to California alone. And California universities' decision to allow Chinese foreign students slots to universities over native Californians made the national news in China.

India: Much of India's rise economically has been because it has dedicated itself to tech support for Western countries. Most of the expertise on running these firms comes from Indians who worked specifically in California's Silicon Valley. Most of the tech firms in India are directly linked through friendship or family connections with workers in Silicon Valley alone. The Times of India routinely reports on California lifestyle in its main news, and the most famous couple in all of India, the actress Aishwarya (Rai) Bachchan and her husband

CALIFORNIA'S NEXT CENTURY 2.0

Abhishek Bachchan, chose to spend their

honeymoon in California.

Brazil: California signed a formal agreement with

Sao Paolo in Brazil to jointly develop technology to

study the effects of climate change in 2005. Brazil

is working a trade deal specifically with California

for the shipment of sugarcane ethanol, which it

hopes can create a new market to boost its economy

to superpower strength.

EU: England's Prime Minister Tony Blair,

specifically commended California and its governor

Schwarzenegger on their climate change work for

its global impact. British newspapers have also

recognized that California has the right to be

independent because America set the precedent of

recognizing Bosnia's right to be independent.[10]

Legalization of Marijuana campaign in California

was big news across the UK. And the major UK

newspaper, *The Guardian*, said that "California has

always been a special place, with its own idea of

what could be achieved in life…It has always been

a place apart."[11] France has specifically been aware

of California since the state won the contest for best

wine in the world held in France. And the EU

climate commissioner met California's governor

personally to see about harmonizing the EU's cap

and trade market specifically to California's in

---

[10] Ed West, "If Kosovo Can Legally Secede from Serbia, What's to Stop Mexifornia Leaving the United States?" *The Telegraph*, July 25, 2010.

[11] In Paul Harris's "Will California become America's first failed state?" *The Guardian*, October 3, 2009, an article discussing if California could overcome its debt crisis of 2010, which it already has.

CALIFORNIA'S NEXT CENTURY 2.0

2011. And again, California was selected as the first site for the UN, has hosted multiple Olympic games, and remains in the top selection lists for where to host future Olympic games.

This is besides the fact that more students from California study abroad than from any other state in America, according to IIE Open Doors Report 2008. California has the largest number of locations for training people to teach English abroad, sixteen as opposed to an average American state's two to four schools. According to Oxfordseminars.com, this means the average US state has 12.5-25% of the amount of people that California has who are interested in traveling and teaching abroad.

Also, the state government already works with private businesses, through the "Buy California Marketing Agreement," to promote a California brand throughout other American states and internationally with the "California grown" advertising campaign since 2002.

As far as other notable influences, "...Hollywood still produces over 80 percent of the world market of films."[12] "Most of the top revenue producers among Hollywood-made movies in the past few years have earned as much or more abroad as in the United States."[13] It should also be noted that America's foreign policy was developed in

---

[12] Abraham Lowenthal, *Global California: Rising to the Cosmopolitan Challenge* (Stanford University Press, 2009), 3.

[13] Ibid., 5.

CALIFORNIA'S NEXT CENTURY 2.0

California first—William Randolph Hearst of San Francisco press was the person who pushed for America to have an expanded foreign role in the late 1800s. The ships for Teddy Roosevelt's Great White fleet, to signify America's rising influence in the world affairs for the first time in its history, were all built in San Francisco. Foreign trade liberalization was pushed by California businessmen first.[14] Additionally, in 1999, California had foreign trade offices in fifteen nations, including all of the future superpowers except Russia, which it added by 2012. Today it has trade offices with thirty-four nations.[15]

---

[14] Ibid., 18–20.

[15] Gus Koehler, *California Trade Policy* (California Research Bureau, 1999).

Second, Switzerland, when it started enacting its role as world political and business nexus, was essentially a subnationally sovereign government to France but was regarded as independent by the world. France basically created the nation of Switzerland during the time of Napoleon, the emperor. A collection of different European nations had lived together for centuries, but the modern government of a unified Switzerland was a creation of Napoleon. Geneva, the negotiation center of the world during its era in Switzerland, is just next to the border with France. This is far away from the Italian, Germany, or Romansch sections of the country, even though German speakers are three-fourths of the nation's population. Furthermore, the original Swiss dollar was based on the value of the French dollar, the franc, the original Swiss dollar was called a Swiss franc. All of this, yet every nation viewed Geneva as impartial and the bank of Switzerland as fair to all nations.

Modern arrangements of subnationally sovereign "type" governments being viewed as independent actors have existed during current times, further establishing the potential for this type of government to be able to be seen as independent. Turkey was militarily linked to the US military for decades: housing many US bases in the Middle East, officers receiving training by America, and accepting a large American military stipend. None of this has changed, yet Turkey is viewed by nations officially hostile to America as an impartial negotiator ever since it publicly forbad America to use the American paid, built, and operated military bases in Turkey for the invasion of Iraq. This one stand against the US military, while changing nothing in the long term, was enough to allow countries such as Iran and Palestine to see Turkey as a fair negotiator in the region. Brazil, at one time in the last couple of decades run by a US-backed dictator, is also seen currently as a fair negotiator in Latin America and international affairs by governments openly hostile to America.

Whoever is the new Switzerland has to achieve sub-national sovereignty for this plan to even work.

The final question is, is it possible for any of these contenders to replace the existing infrastructure and long-term historical reputation already obtained by

CALIFORNIA'S NEXT CENTURY 2.0

Switzerland? As stated before, the world is already making new negotiation centers in different regions that are not connected to the old powers or negotiation centers, so the replacement has already started. The fact that many of these new centers— EU, WTO, G20, ASEAN, MERCOSUR—have existed for over a decade (some approaching two decades) and continue to hold numerous meetings, shows that they are not fleeting trends that will pass but rather the birth of something that will only continue to grow. These new centers show that A) the world is pulling away from Switzerland already, and permanently, and will increase its distance, and B) that others can develop the level of international linking and sophistication in negotiation that Switzerland has.

Also important is the historical fact that Switzerland was not the first place to develop a nexus of international negotiation skills. It was London, England, from the late 1700s to 1850. When Switzerland copied London institutions, such as meeting halls and universities specializing in international diplomacy, it began to mature. So the existence of Switzerland as we know it proves that the international negotiation center skill set can be learned by others to the point of replacing the original masters and innovators.

CALIFORNIA'S NEXT CENTURY 2.0

CHAPTER 5: WHY CALIFORNIA WOULD WANT TO BE MOSTLY INDEPENDENT

The following would be possible specifically because of the new powers granted from independence and would not be possible without this independence.

Living Standards Improve:

- For the last century, Switzerland has been routinely ranked as having the highest quality of life in the world because of the income generated from its unique market. From 1800 to 2000, Switzerland's living standard was always above or equal to the largest nations that dwarf it in size.

CALIFORNIA'S NEXT CENTURY 2.0

- Related to this, Switzerland's economy has been strong and growing almost every year since 1850. There have been periods of recession, for a few years, but the trend has always been of secure economic growth—again because of its unique global position for certain internationally in-demand services.

- Also, for its tiny size, Switzerland has had the global influence of the giant superpowers that meet there, never through direct means, but through indirection persuasion. Instead it has been able to imprint its global view "weltanschauung" to the same effectiveness as England, America, Russia, France, and China. Some nations will only deal with Switzerland and not directly with superpowers (such as Iran and, before that, the USSR).

- California would gain around seventy billion dollars instantly, or the equivalent of one full state budget.

- Only a small fraction of this money would be needed to buy off California's current deficit. Another fraction could be used to create a savings account that would grow with interest to a size large enough to float the entire state budget in the next recession in the future.

- Also this money would allow California to fix the state's infrastructure—roads, airports, dams, levees, rivers, public buildings, schools—which all are in the lowest performance of all fifty states, according to the Federal government itself.

- Could allow gay marriage and full rights for gay people, such as immigration, which is not allowed in America.

- Could ban discrimination against Muslims, which is legal and practiced by the American government in America. Rights would be instituted for all persons of Muslim faith, rather than the illegal spying admitted by the FBI, as seen especially in New York City.

- Could allow immigration from Caribbean nations with African descendants. This would increase the African descendant population in California, making it larger but also richer in experience.

CALIFORNIA'S NEXT CENTURY 2.0

- Could allow immigration from traditional matriarchal cultures to increase the number of people who see women as natural leaders living in California.

- Could grant a reservation to all tribes in California. Many of the recognized tribes and many officially unrecognized federal tribes still do not have a reservation. Allocating land from the Sierra Mountains to claim as their own, the reservations would be small like the size of the Tule reservation, but all natives would formally receive a sovereign piece of territory.

CALIFORNIA'S NEXT CENTURY 2.0

California Government Will Become More Effective:

- Although the new government would not control the dollar, it could control banking practices of all banks within California. It could prevent: bad loans from being sold, bad loans from being packaged together, or bad loans from being sold without being disclosed up front. And it could issue heavy financial punishments for all businesses that participate in these forms of banking.

- California left all of the faith in protecting its economy to federal experts, all of whom say that they totally missed all warning signs for years that led to the giant, global-wide financial collapse. Overlooking the creation of a giant economic catastrophe of this scale is simply not wise. The federal government, of its own admittance, has said that every single economic overseer of all checks on the economy missed the warning signs.[16] California should therefore create its own watchdog agency for watching and warning the public of specific, potential negative economic trends. The faith of protecting the economy could be placed in an agency focused on California and be provided with the power to at least influence California banks directly.

- Most of the Californian government receives funding for all of the different actions that it does from the federal government in a series

[16] Robert J. Shiller, "Economic View: Challenging the Crowd in Whispers Not Shouts", *The New Yorker*, November 1, 2008

of specialized grants. All of this money requires accounting. California agencies have to spend time packaging their requests for funding to the federal government, the federal government has to review the state's paperwork, then another agency issue the grants, then another state agency has to receive the federal grants and split them up to fund all of the state activities. With no federal oversight on state government, all of this oversight can be cut. The government of the state can simply do the actions that need done directly instead of waiting for approval and having to figure out the approval process. Government will shrink and simplify.

- Additionally, most of the brightest
  California citizens who work in government
  or related private sector fields leave
  California to go to Washington, DC, to work
  in the highest level their careers can achieve.
  With the California government being the
  highest level for careers in government,
  more of top talent will stay in the state,
  improving the effectiveness of government.

It Will Be Possible for California to be the Greatest It Can Be:

- Having the ability to effectively decide all
  aspects of its governance will give
  Californians the ability, for the first time
  ever, to be in full control of their destiny.
  They could design a nation that fits their

particular sensibilities instead of designing a government that reaches to California's sensibilities but within the confines of forty-nine other states' opinions on what should be legal or what the proper role of government is. In fact, one of the main reasons that Scotland asked for sub-regional sovereignty from England was to be the most Scottish that they could be without worrying about laws and actions of the government fitting in with other UK states. Since 1850 California has embodied a different culture and behaved in a different cultural gravity source than the rest of America—and the rest of Mexico. What science, ideas, art, music, videos, new inventions, world views, philosophy, poetry, and fashion styles will take over in California if the people felt that they really did have the ability to design their government to whatever fit for them? This freedom is one they've never had and yet have consistently displayed a unique culture despite of. What happens when that last border is taken away?

Examples abound of the federal government limiting California. Stem cell research was pioneered in California but stopped by the federal government for years. Climate change legislation was the same story, also pioneered in California, and stalled for years by the federal government.[17]

---

[17] Jennifer Lance, "Schwarzenegger Angry with Bush over Global Warming Inaction," Red Blue and Green, July 16, 2008; Kathleen Sebelius and Ned Sebelius, *Bearing the Burden of*

CALIFORNIA'S NEXT CENTURY 2.0

President Obama traveled to California to promise that the federal government would not police marijuana use, then a year later, the federal government started policing marijuana use.[18] California is a land where the right to marry someone of the same sex is acceptable and where women have the right to choose to get an abortion, yet these rights are constantly threatened in every federal presidential election.[19]

- It would be the first nation in our era to be a land of true equality. California has many social problems, and racism and direct

---

the Beltway: Practical Realities of State Government and Federal-State Relations in the Twenty-First Century, Harvard Law and Policy Review, Vol 3 (2009)

[18] Anthony Gregory, "Will Obama Stop the Medical Marijuana Raids?" *Campaign for Liberty*, January 29, 2009.

[19] Chris Moody, "Seven Ways Rick Perry Wants to Change the Constitution," *yahoo.com*, August 19, 2011

xenophobia still exist, but California is possibly closest to true equality of humanity anywhere in the world. It's the closest to a place where a person can have any background and be treated only by the content of their character and abilities. If California had A) the ability to shape society as it saw fit locally, B) the mantel, C) the public understanding that it had this ability, and D) a calling to do this, it is entirely possibly that Californians could achieve a society in a relatively short time that was the image of pure equality—a society where people were judged only on ability alone. Immigration would be one of the key powers California would hold to achieve this. It could seek to balance and maintain a diverse array of cultures—to enact "a land

of minorities," following the phrase "a land

of minorities is a land where there are no

minorities." It is a very old saying unable to

trace, but the truth it holds is current. In a

land where everyone is a segment of the

population, they learn to respect each other

equally, live together, intermarry, befriend,

work together, and build great societies.

Switzerland (German, Italian, French,

Romansch), Lebanon (before the invasion

by Israel turned it from the "Paris of the

Middle East," as the world once referred to

it, into the war zone it is today), Israel

(European, Middle Eastern, Russian,

American, Ethiopian), and Singapore

(Chinese, Malaysian, British, Indian) are all

examples. From these examples we can see that people who live on a geographic island (separated by mountains or waters) that is beautiful and who have a strong sense that it is a special place, develop a joint community out of a group of minorities—because they are all minorities.

Raw Economics

- California's economy is linked to foreign trade and foreign relations in general by about 25%, or one-fourth, of the total state's economy: the movement of international services and goods through California employees directly is about one-fifth of the economy, and one-fourth of the state's population is born outside of America.

Compared to other states, where only one-tenth of the economy is linked to foreign trade and only one-tenth of the population of only some states is foreign born, California's link to the global world is in a class by itself.[20] Fareed Zakaria states, "But actually, the American economy is quite insular; exports account for only about 10% of it."[21] In California, 50% of all foreign investment was from Asia alone, whereas it was only 30% of investment in America. California's amount of exports surpasses the next ten states in America's

---

[20] "Chamber Highlights Jobs Fallout from Anti-Outsourcing Legislation," CalChamber, 2004.

[21] Fareed Zakaria, "US Decline in Global Arena: Is America No Longer No. 1?" *Time,* March 3, 2011.

exports combined.[22] (Also see Appendix V.) This has caused problems because the federal government routinely holds up foreign trade deals and other foreign relations issues that are much more pressing for the state of California than for the rest of America. **The former governor of California literally pleaded with multiple presidents of the federal government of America to pass trade deals that had been signed with traditional American allies but had been stalled in Washington for years.**[23] This should not be a surprise:

---

[22] Gus Koehler, *California Trade Policy* (California Research Bureau, 1999), 12.

[23] Kelly Olsen, "Schwarzenegger: Congress Stalling On Free Trade Agreements," Huffington Post, 2010; Clyde Prestowitz, "Washington Doesn't Sincerely Want Jobs," Foreign Policy, 2011; "Schwarzenegger Urges Congress to Ratify Free Trade

California pleaded with the federal government to pass the first world trade agreement in 1994 (almost twenty years earlier) with GATT and "was the only state to provide US negotiators to the GATT with detailed country and industry sector reports on trade barriers and potential GATT impact to business." Basic material that America would need to make the trade deal worthwhile was only provided by California.[24]

Deals at End of Asian Tour," Topix.com, 2010; Martha C. White, "Blue Diamond Growers: What a California Almond Company Can Teach Us About the Globalization of American Agriculture," Slate.com, 2010; "Failed South Korean Trade Deal a Setback for Obama," Cleveland.com, 2010.

[24] "California World Trade Commission urges passage of GATT," Business Wire, 1994; Niels Erich, "California's Trade Program: A Model State-Federal Partnership—Includes Information on Export Finance Services; Trade Contacts;

International trade negotiations are just not that important to the rest of America as they are to California. Because all international trade and other international relations have to be worked out at the federal level, California is routinely set up to just wait and suffer and hope while its economy significantly suffers. According to Michael Porter, "Relative to most nations, the US has a cumbersome structure for formulating and implementing trade policy...Trade policy is usually ad hoc, set through responding to individual cases."[25] In addition, Abraham Lowenthal contends that "...a long standing

---

Cresset Powers, an Export Trading Company," Business America, 1989.

[25] Michael Porter, *The Competitive Advantage of Nations* (The Free Press, 1990), 733.

but inadequately understood and therefore often ignored reality—that international trends, events, relationships and policies greatly affect California and its distinct regions, and that Californians therefore have important international interests."[26] Lowenthal states, "Although Californians have important international policy interests, we do not have systemic ways to identify, rank and pursue them."[27] Lowenthal concludes that "Californians have important international interests but cannot pursue most of them effectively

---

[26] Abraham Lowenthal, *Global California: Rising to the Cosmopolitan Challenge* (Stanford University Press, 2009), 80.

[27] Ibid., 81.

through state public policies."[28]

The situation for California is that it is hurt by the federal government not placing the same importance on international trade on ideas, money, jobs, and goods that California places in general. In addition, the federal government's willingness to upset the entire world with foreign affairs (as described at the very beginning of this report) hurts the level of international trade, cooperation, investment, and flow of ideas that California's economy depends on. California feels losses in tourism, college students, foreign investment, and willingness to sign trade deals at a whole other level—much more significantly than

---

[28] Ibid., 125.

America—because it is much more
dependent on international trade and
relations than other American states. In 2005
the government of California issued a report
showing how just the loss of international
students was particularly damaging to the
entire California higher education system
and, actually, the entire state's long-term
economy.[29]

• Federal income taxes and state income taxes
  would become combined, as the state would
  increase state income taxes to cover new
  roles that were previously federal roles.
  However, this would simplify the tax effort

---

[29] Todd Giedt, *The Critical Decline in International: Graduate Student Enrollments* (University of California, 2005).

of all businesses and individuals. Secondly, the seventy billion in tax money that would not be taken out of California could directly go into lowering the overall corporate income tax rate. Theoretically it would be possible to make the independent nation of California's business tax rate at the same level as Hong Kong and Singapore—the most competitive corporate tax rates of any nation in the world. This would thrust California's business climate to the top of competitiveness worldwide for the first time, possibly ever. (Also see Appendix V.)

- Currently federal income taxes are filed by California people, sent to the federal government where it is reviewed, and then processed by another federal agency into grants that are sent back to the California to use, which have to be processed by state government workers. Eliminating the federal tax level removes multiple agencies of government that oversee this loop of finance, and the cost of running all of the government bureaucracy at the federal and state levels for processing state-originated federal income taxes can go back to the taxpayers and help to further reduce the corporate tax rate.

- During the last twenty-five years, California has never been helped out during a recession by the federal government regardless of whether a liberal Democrat or conservative

Republican was president. During the last fifteen years, California has had to pay for all of its goods movement infrastructure despite the fact that it is the port for all of American foreign goods; and it has to pay for all of the costs of disaster assistance for floods and wildfires. **The whole point of a Federal union is to create a large pot of resources that everyone can pull from at different times to help their smaller government out. California never receives help from the federal point, thus denying the entire point of federalism.** (Also see Appendix I.)

CHAPTER 6: WHY AMERICA WOULD WANT THIS AND NOT BE OPPOSED TO IT

In this chapter we'll examine the benefits of this new arrangement for America.

- America does not change anything else it is doing because of this plan. It adds the actions of this plan to its existing policies and institutions. However, the world is changing and some American developed and resourced global agencies will likely fall dramatically in popularity. This plan provides America a way to compensate for this seemingly inevitable change.

- This will be a globally recognized, positive news event—at a time when America most needs positive press in its history.

- The Federal government will run more
  effectively without dealing with California's
  issues. California is so incredibly different
  from the main population of America in
  social concerns and business issues. This
  routinely makes making decisions in
  America more complicated because either
  things that work for most of the country
  don't work in California or Californians just
  don't like the solution that works for the rest
  of America. Decisions will be easier to make
  and faster without considering California.
  This is the reason why the American
  government has already given control over
  insurance, environmental law, and health

care law (three of the most complicated

arenas of government) to California while it

has retained these powers for other states.

Furthermore, new research suggests that a

smaller government will automatically

increase business activity. By shrinking the

burden of governing, the health of the

American economy will grow.[1]

Furthermore, the American people already

consider the size of the federal government

too large. CNN conducted a poll that

---

[1] Rob Salmond, *Governments and Growth: Size Matters* (University of Michigan, 2006); Diana Cook, Carsten Schousboe, and David Law, "Government and Economic Growth: Does size matter?" New Zealand Treasury Department (2011); Ruta Aidis, "Size Matters: Entrepreneurial Entry and Government," University College London, 2010; Ilya Somin, "Why the Size of Government Matters," 2009.

showed almost 60% of all Americans, including nearly 40% of liberals, think that the American national government is already too big because it does not deal with their issues effectively or deals with them too slowly.[2] The American public is not incorrect in feeling this way; since 2000 to 2010, the federal government has expanded significantly in size.[3]

- In every single world body, China has two voices that constantly talk about Chinese

---

[2] *"Poll: Government is Way Too Big"*, Back Bench Media, March 3, 2010, http://www.backbenchmedia.com/poll-government-big/

[3] Kathleen Sebelius and Ned Sebelius, "Bearing the Burden of the Beltway: Practical Realities of State Government and Federal-State Relations in the Twenty-First Century." (Harvard Law and Policy review, vol 3, 2009)

issues but are seen by the world as two different peoples. The world sees these two peoples as different, and so it views these issues as legitimate instead of as issues just being pushed by Chinese peoples. The world gives legitimacy to Hong Kong as a separate people with their own mindset, so when Hong Kong talks about something that China does, the entire world listens as if it is a natural consensus forming. England is now achieving the same situation in international presence with Scotland and France is with New Caledonia. Because it would not be America holding an idea alone, but seen as a consensus of what to do, many programs that America wants to enact on the world stage would have a much greater chance of being accepted in the world. If California is seen as the one presenting a Latin nation trading league instead of America, it has a greater chance of selling just because it's not America pushing the idea (although America is part of it). Recently, in 2012, America learned this lesson with the war on Libya, where America liked the idea and greatly aided the war, but the Europeans pushed the idea to the world stage. The president knew that, right or wrong, it would be viewed as an American war, instead of the right thing to do, and would hurt the support for an invasion of Libya. "Leading from behind" was the phrase that America used to have the Europeans lead the fight into a war that was principally supplied by

America.

Given the existing strong international presence of California, American ideas will be spread far without being seen as American. Furthermore, the idea of having a newly independent state become the chief spokesperson to improve America's standing in an area has already been suggested. In the *New York Times*, Michael Janeway suggested that Puerto Rico can help lead the Latin America area in developing a way to meet US goals including how to plan a Latin American region that is democratic once Fidel Castro dies. America has been unable to get Latin American countries to do this mostly because they listen to Fidel

Castro's argument that America is not to be trusted since it still holds Puerto Rico as a colony.[4]

- With the new change, the American dollar will become stronger. For example, although large and established, **England may have only been able to stay independent from the EU with its currency because of the help of the smaller but more vibrant and much faster growing economy of Ireland, which also held the British pound.** Without Ireland as a separate but still-in-the-English-family nation, England may not have been strong enough to hold onto its

---

[4] Michael Janeway, "Puerto Rico's Moment in the Sun," *New York Times*, May 22, 2008.

British pound and would had to have followed almost every other nation in Europe in adopting the EU currency.

China has a similar story with Hong Kong. Both are Chinese nations but have very different historical cultures related to the economy. China is able to attract foreign money and talent and be seen as serious about business (which helped convince many foreigners to invest their money in China) because China did not try to overrun Hong Kong but recognized its independence and let it stay independent. Because of this move, the Chinese economy is stronger and growing faster and has more foreign investment. All of which means that the

Chinese yuan is growing faster into a place of global dominance because of how it treated Hong Kong and because Hong Kong uses the same currency as China.

Malaysia's ringgit owes a similar debt to Singapore and Brunei for using its dollar and being innovative countries. France owes a similar debt to Switzerland and Lichtenstein for the same. Belarus has also helped keep the Russian ruble viewed as more of an international currency. The small economy of American colonies provided a similar role of strength to the Mexican peso until after the Constitution was signed in early American history. Today, Panama and Costa Rica provide a similar role for the US dollar in Latin America. Qatar, UAE, until 1973, provided a similar role for the Saudi Arabian riyal.

- Better domestic debate would result from the change. Many political experts on both conservative and liberal sides have remarked that political debate has degenerated into "slogans and shouting" and the actual debate has been removed. Politicians who actually debate instead of sticking to just a few messages can no longer win in America. This is largely California's fault. California has been called "the west" of America, the edge of social concepts and progressive, American-style philosophies. However, because of the separation of the populations of California from the main American population by half the

nation's length (a distance equal to that of

between Chinese culture and Russian, European

culture and Middle Eastern, Indian culture and

Chinese, South American culture and North

American) there is a large disconnect. (Also see

Appendix I.)

Ideas that are progressive become effectively

radicalized in California, to an extreme that is

too harsh for the main culture of America to

absorb. In the 1960s, in the main American

population Martin Luther King preached from

the Bible about nonviolence and reaching out to

white middle-class voters. At the exact same

time in California, the Black Panther

organization formed, preaching violence first in

order to achieve equality, and it did not reach out to white middle-class voters but attempted to physically intimidate them. Both organizations had legitimate grievances, but they dealt with them very differently. Violent Black-nationalists organizations did occur in MAP, but they never spread and they died out quickly. The Black Panthers ideology spread out across America and was not received well in the main American population.

Today, in 2011, the main American population is still debating if people can get married if they are gay. California has already married thousands of people and has at least two gay majority metropolitan regions (West Hollywood and Castro District). The marrying of gay men

256

in San Francisco set off a firestorm of controversy in MAP: many state governments angrily denounced gay marriage and set up new laws, and hate crimes against Gay people in MAP rose. Desegregation started in California in the thirties, but it didn't happen in America until the late fifties. The environmental movement and health care are other examples of ideas that started and saturated California on average twenty to thirty years before the main American population was socially accepting of similar ideas.

Those were positive examples used to prove the reach of California culture to infest the ideology of MAP, but they prove the negative examples are just as likely to spread. The first motorcycle outlaw gang that started the entire outlaw motorcycle drug-running culture was the Hells

Angeles, founded in Hollister in California. The

Bloods and Crips, two national gangs of every

inner city in America, both started in Los

Angeles, California. Mara Sepeltrucha, the most

violent gang in America and spreading to all

Latino communities in MAP, started in Los

Angeles. Nazi Lowriders and Aryan

brotherhood, two of the most violent white

supremacists gangs across America, started in

California in San Quinton and Pelican Bay

prisons, respectively. Some of the most violent

criminal organizations, the Mexican Mafia and

Black Guerilla Family, also started in California

prisons and spread east. The violent music genre

of gangster rap, where lyrics routinely talk about

negatively using women and committing

violence, started in Los Angeles by Jewish record company industry veteran Jerry Heller through the introduction of the group NWA to the music listening public. It was further spread years later by the music recording label Death Row Records led by Suge Knight and rapper Snoop Dogg. After it started in California, gangster rap appeared in New York and the rest of the country (although the original art form of rap started in New York City).

In summary, California introduces radical ideas into America that are rejected by America, or cause much social problems in America, because they were ideas formed to fit an entirely different culture. National protestant Christian televangelists listened to by a majority of the main American population constantly talk about new bad ideas coming from California to their communities and to "watch out." Politicians backed this up, focusing on anti-gay marriage and anti-climate change legislation to win elections after these ideas were pioneered in California. States are shipping their money to California to affect California debates instead of spending that money on debates in their states because they are afraid of the coming of California ideas (Louisiana spent millions to affect the California climate change bill, and Utah spent millions to affect the gay marriage rights legislation). Instead of having debates and calm language and spending money on their local affairs, California has caused a fear in the main American population. The result is more short, stunted rhetoric, more shouting, less debate, increased fear, and less resources (attention, time, and money) in states on America's local issues. California is too separated from MAP to be the progressive testing ground for America.

Here's the proof: all of the progressive movements that happened in America before 1950 (when California started booming as a population after WWII, before which it was very rural compared to the rest of MAP) happened on the western edge of the existing boundaries of MAP (close to the I-35 freeway). Where they were the furthest geographic distance from the center of decisions in Washington, DC, but were still physically connected directly to the entire American population. Evolution being taught in schools was literally fought over not in California but in Kansas City. Communists being able to run for top government office happened in Milwaukee. These were radical ideas at their time, and they all happened on this western edge—not in California. The height of technology during this same period was not in California but in Houston, Texas, where the mission to put a man on the moon was planned out since the late-1950s. A decade later in the 1960s, America got the first taste of California progressivism: hippies, people who dropped acid to drop out of society, Black Panthers, Brown Berets, Helter Skelter. These concepts shocked MAP when they spread there, and there has been a cultural battle ever since. Although the Scopes trial and Eugene V. Debs were at the very edge of society, they did not cause the shock and outrage to MAP that radical concepts from California did. This is because the ideas from Kansas City and Milwaukee were filtered correctly for a MAP instead of filtered for a different type of population who did not regularly connect with MAP. The reaction to government oppression in the 1950s and 1960s, the "liberal movement" or "civil rights era," should have taken place in MAP, not in California—it would have resulted in reform that was less radical and more in tune with the population they were trying to influence.

A progressive West that returns to the borders of MAP will end the crazy debates and allow progressive ideas to still filter into America. But debate will return, calm talk will return, working together among parties will return,

focusing attention and all money on local issues

will return once the polarization resulting from

too-radical California ideas being directly

injected into MAP has been removed.

Furthermore, at the same time the world is

rapidly changing in dramatic ways. America has

taken on more non-northern European

immigrants than in its entire history. Its rate of

immigration is equal to the rate of the 1930s, but

during that era, the immigrants primarily came

from a common European culture. Today's

immigrant dynamic does not have the same

situation. America needs cultural cohesion now

more than ever. It needs to merge many very

different cultural peoples into a common

CALIFORNIA'S NEXT CENTURY 2.0

American identity at a time when America's role in the world is changing. When other great societies faced similar eras of massive global change, they sought to return to a "sense of themselves" in order to keep their large nations together. This happened with England in the late 1800s as the Second Industrial Revolution started, and with China in the 1960s as a post-WWII global economy began to emerge. America, more than ever before, needs to simplify its domestic debate and discussion on what it is to be an American, and keeping California part of that debate will only aggravate and complicate the debate, confusing immigrants who should be assimilating.

- This does not mean that an independent California can't serve as a filter for America still. Many of the best filters for new ideas in business and socially, for large nations, come from independent smaller nations. Hong Kong still produces most of the movies and business investment models for China. UAE pioneered tourism in the Middle East and innovative Muslim-oriented banking. Brussels is home of all of the debates of what should happen to the rest of Europe. When Japan was isolated from the world most of the new ideas entered into Japan through the island of Dejima, which was cut off from mainland Japan physically and in communications. Ireland pioneered new financial economic models for England. Maldives is seen as a pioneer of issues for India being the first to deal with climate change issues. The official monitor of the Indian Ocean Commission, Brazil, looks to Uruguay as the pioneer for international trade and finance. Africa has Cape Verde to try out new European business and legal models on an African-type cultured country. Because these smaller nations are close, but not connected and not of the same government, they are able to experiment with policies more flexibly than much larger governments. Because of the government disconnect and physical distance, they are able to be watched safely from afar by the neighboring nations to see what trends they like and which ones they don't and specifically pick which trends they want to allow to be imported into their own countries.

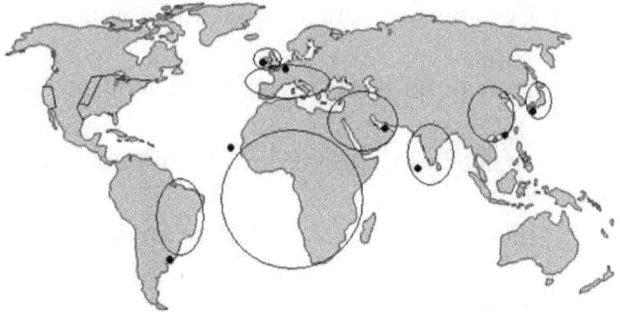

Dot = filter nation

Circle = larger nation

Squares with white sprinkles = two filter regions

of America, current and historic.

- Specifically the elites of America will want

   this plan as it better achieves their long-

   running goals for the world by leaps ahead

   of their current efforts. During WWII, super

   wealthy families in America like the

CALIFORNIA'S NEXT CENTURY 2.0

Rockefellers developed the Council on Foreign Relations in New York City. All foreign diplomats and all foreign relations thinkers are trained here and are members. This small fraternity of internationally trained thinkers routinely meets and debates ways to ensure American power in the world and world peace in general.

There's one main reason that the California's Next Century (CNC) plan can supply their long-term dream by multiple orders of magnitude more than they could have ever organized. While the elites have at best gathered together brilliant minds of a few hundred people to think about how to achieve a global order, California would be a living example of it happening day to day among brilliant people and regular people. In this living experiment, a multitude of different, varied, richer, and more brilliant ideas will be created as only a "cloud computing" or living "wiki network" could do. A cloud computer network is more brilliant than a smaller group of only the most brilliant people because there is a wider range of ideas, and yet there is still brilliance within the cloud to work out ideas. The proof: scientists for decades literally have been trying to understand the AIDS virus—how it works and why it is so hard to kill and easily spread. This year, for fun, a video game online chat room competed to make a model of the AIDS virus. Within two months, using the cloud mind, for fun, video gamers developed a working model of the AIDS virus, allowing scientists to understand specifically what they were dealing with. In contrast the best scientists in the world were not able to develop a working AIDS virus model in nearly twenty years of heavily funded research.[5]

- The biggest reason is no other state in America or nation in the world could enact the role of Switzerland for the next century, not all or even remotely. If America wants a peaceful, orderly transition into the next

---

[5] "Plugged In: Online Gamers Crack AIDS Enzyme Puzzle," *Associated Foreign Press,* September 19, 2011.

century, it will have to support this proposal.

- **Furthermore, America will not be shocked at all by the idea of a separate California.** It has always thought of California as different from the rest of the country, and it has heard this stated publicly by government officials for decades. In 1860, President Lincoln was informed that the Californians thought of themselves as different from Americans and maybe, just years after joining the Union, they should leave it. He rushed to build the transcontinental railroad to better connect California and to avoid a secession war on two fronts. In 1862, California was the only state to reject the official national war

currency of the greenbacks.[6] Theodore
Roosevelt publicly called California a
strange place, saying it was "west of the
west" in the early 1900s.[7] Historian Carey
McWilliams described California as "a
freak" in the 1940s.[8] McWilliams further
went on to say that, "While politically
California was a part of the union," ...
"geographically she was an isolated
community separated from the central
government by thousands of miles ...it was
this feeling...that gave rise to a serious

---

[6] Brad Skiles, "California Leads Nation with Sound Money—in 1865," Misses Daily, 2010, http://mises.org/daily/4625

[7] David Shafie, H. Schockman, and *Matthew Cahn, Rethinking California: Politics and Policy in the Golden State* (Prentice Hall, 2001), 1.

[8] Ibid., 11.

secessionist movement."[9] Moreover, "For the first twenty years of statehood—Californians never thought of themselves as Americans but as a separate culture. The largest proof of the strength of the culture was the speed of which 'Okies' were Californian-ized in short time. The 'past' means to the Californians not the Pilgrim fathers, or William Penn and the Indians, or George Washington crossing the Delaware...the historically minded Californian of today is orientated with reference to a set of meanings and significances quite unlike those by which the historically minded in other areas, even in the West, guide their research and historical

---

[9] Ibid., 55.

explorations."[10] McWilliams also wrote, "Preoccupied with its peculiar problems, isolated from the rest of the nation…in its early history, California develops a remarkable energy and resourcefulness in the solution of its problems without consultation or assistance from other western states or the Federal government."[11]

Edmund "Pat" Brown, a former governor of California who almost ran for the presidency of America, stated in the 1960s, "California is part and apart from the larger American society. It is both representative and

[10] Ibid., 60–61.

[11] Carey McWilliams, *California: The Great Exception* (UC Press, 1940), 364.

unique.'"[12] Around the same time, Curt Gentry describes California as the evil version of America.[13] Also, popular comedians expressed these sentiments about California: "...Woody Allen's crack that turning right on red was California's only cultural contribution and Johnny Carson's quip that the only live culture in California was its yogurt."[14]

Consider that "...California's Assembly pushed in 2007 for a statewide referendum on 'whether the President should end the US occupation of

---

[12] Dale Maharidge, *The Coming White Minority: California's' Eruption and the Nation's Future* (Crown, 1996), 9.

[13] Curt Gentry, *The Last Days of the Late Great State of California* (Comstock Book distributors, 1968), 385–387.

[14] Abraham Lowenthal, *Global California: Rising to the Cosmopolitan Challenge*, (Stanford University Press, 2009), 31.

Iraq.' Some three hundred towns across the
country had adopted measures to this effect, but
no state had yet done so."[15] When the state
asked for a financial bailout in 2008, people
from main population of America made
numerous calls on the Internet for California to
just leave. Popular national radio personality
Laura Ingraham, tired of California's insistence
on climate change, suggested on air that
California "just secede already."[16]

The opinion has continued. In 2004, the book
Politics and Government in California authors
David Provost and Bernard Hyink said that

---

[15] Ibid., 124.

[16] "Ingraham Rails Against Schwarzenegger, Tells California:
'Just Secede Already,'" *Think Progress,* November 11, 2008.

America considered California as two-thirds
"bad" and "ugly" and described it as "nuts,"
"eccentric," "lala land," and "gross."[17] In 2010,
the Heritage Foundation asked, "Outside the
Beltway: What Country is California in Again?"
(by Conn Carroll). The *National Review*
concluded that California is just a different kind
of state in "What Happened in California?"
(by John J. Pitney, 2010). A year prior an
academic review of California concluded that
"...because national foreign policymakers
tend to think of California as remote and

---

[17] David Provost and Bernard Hyink, *Politics and Government in California* (Longman, 2006), 1, 11.

exotic, if not irrelevant."[18]

- The proposal that is being asked for is
  nothing other than what the federal
  government has directly suggested should
  happen to the island of Puerto Rico.
  President Obama and President George W.
  Bush before him, have said that Puerto Rico
  should vote on if it wants to stay a territory,
  become fully independent, or become a state
  of the US, but that the decision would be
  taken by a planned, heavily debated vote in
  2012. They said that Puerto Rico should
  have this vote because it was a national

---

[18] Abraham Lowenthal, *Global California: Rising to the Cosmopolitan Challenge*, (Stanford University Press, 2009), xiii.

government that had been taken over by

military force by America.

(Also see Appendix I and Appendix IV.)

CALIFORNIA'S NEXT CENTURY 2.0

CHAPTER 7: CALIFORNIA COULD

ACHIEVE THIS AND THEN SOME

NEW WORLD ORDER?

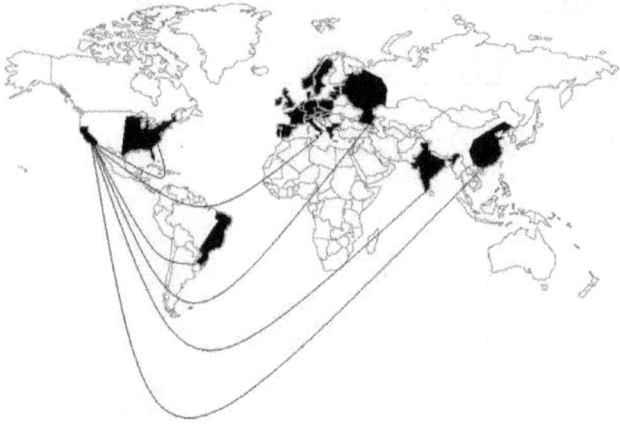

The future?

Besides already having the education, trade, and infrastructure facilities to serve as the nexus for the world for the next century, why would Californians want to take on this position? Because they have already been talking about it. There have been multiple movements for California to be its own country over the last two hundred years, right up to ten years ago:

CALIFORNIA'S NEXT CENTURY 2.0

- 1849: The "Californios" wanted to become a separate state from Mexico but were beaten by the "Bear Flaggers" who created an independent California republic with its own president for a very short time.

- 1850: Republic of Rough and Ready was declared an independent country in California.

- 1860: President Abraham Lincoln ordered the construction of the transcontinental railroad because he heard that California-Americans were talking about becoming their own nation again after just joining the American government, and he did not want to fight a secession war on two fronts.

- 1930: President FDR recognized that California needed its own currency and instructed the federal reserve to devise a system where California would be its own "currency area."

- 1941: The "Republic of Jefferson" in California declared secession and actually manned armed checkpoints to announce their position.

- 1970: The book *Ecotopia*, a big seller in California, talked about the separation of California and Oregon from the rest of America.

- 2005: The California chapter of the "Move On" political organization announced an investigation into making California secede from America because of the election of George W. Bush; the "Committee to

Explore Secession" was headed by Jeff Morrissette.

In the last few years, multiple state legislators (Jackie Spier, Dick Lovejoy, Able Maldonado, and Governor Arnold Schwarzenegger) have complained about the amount of money that California contributes to the federal government without seeing an equal return in services. They have alluded that California should take back some or a lot of its policy independence. And there is a formal petition online for this, already with 1,200 signatures as of this writing.[1]

---

[1] "A Petition for California's Secession from the Federal Government" accessed May 3, 2012, http://www.petitiononline.com/casec/petition.html.

But California's interest in independence does not stop at informal movements. The official government has formally made moves in the last couple of decades. The government has run foreign trade offices from the 1960s throughout Asian and Latin America. **In recent decades, it has ordered multiple official reports looking into California's global position and investigating what a separate foreign policy should look like.**[2] Researchers have independently proposed a foreign policy for California in academic publications in 1990 and

---

[2] *California State Government and the Global Economy* (Cal Trade Report, 2004); Howard Shatz, "Business Without Borders? Assessing the Globalization of the California Economy, PPIC," 2003; "Need for Legislative Oversight in Global Economy," 2000 (This looks at California's role in the WTO); Gus Koehler, "California Trade Policy," 1999; Nick Vucinich, "Tapping New Markets: California's Role in Promoting International Trade," 1993; Leo McCarthy, "International Trade Policy for California," 1986.

CALIFORNIA'S NEXT CENTURY 2.0

2000.[3] Taking it a step further, nonacademic

individuals have released reports looking at what

a future independent California might look like in

general.[4]

Specifically the government has already said that it

should use its ethnic population to establish links to

the home countries of its immigrants for business

---

[3] James Goldsborough, "California Foreign Policy," 1993;
Robert Collier, "California on the Global High Road: State
Trade and Investment Strategy for the 21st Century," 1999;
Cynthia A. Kroll, Dwight M. Jaffee, Ashok Deo Bardhan, Josh
Kirschenbaum, and David K. Howe, "Foreign Trade and
California's Economic Growth. A Policy Research Program
Report," 1998; Abraham Lowenthal, *Global California: Rising
to the Cosmopolitan Challenge* (2009).

[4] Alfred E. Heller, *The California Tomorrow Plan* (1972); Kim
Stanley Robinson, *Three Californias* Trilogy (Pacific Edge, Wild
Shore, Gold Coast) (released in sections in 1989, 1991, 2003).

and politics.[5]

Since 2002 the state government has worked in partnership with private export businesses to develop national (among the other forty-nine states) and international California brand name recognition with the "California Grown" campaign. Furthermore, the same governor who started that program was scolded by the Federal President of America, George W. Bush, for traveling to Asia and making separate trade deals with different nations directly, a duty reserved for the federal government. However, none of these trade deals have been called off and instead have been left standing. But this sort of stance

---

[5] Gus Koehler, *California Trade Policy* (California Research Bureau, 1999), 67, 69.

goes back nearly fifty years, **Governors Pat Brown, Ronald Reagan, Jerry Brown, George Deukmejian, Pete Wilson, Grey Davis, and Arnold Schwarzenegger all called for expanded free trade and traveled to foreign countries directly to promote it. In addition Assembly Speaker Willie Brown created the California World Trade Commission, and Assembly Speaker Robert Hertzog created the Office of Protocol and International. Mayors Tom Bradley, Richard Riordan, Jim Hahn, Antonio Villarigosa, and Diane Feinstein personally promoted international trade relations for their cities.**[6]

---

[6] Abraham Lowenthal, *Global California: Rising to the Cosmopolitan Challenge* (Stanford University Press, 2009), 38–41.

CALIFORNIA'S NEXT CENTURY 2.0

Since 1998, Michael Milken, the international finance manager, has held "Global Conferences" in Los Angeles, where leaders from around the world in business and science are brought together. Also, every year, the richest business leaders from around the world are invited to meet north of San Francisco in "Bohemian Grove" to network with each other. Furthermore, the federal government has sought California's unique ability to forecast global trends. The National Intelligence Council for America in 2008 asked a California-based consulting company, SRIC-BI, to conduct an investigation, resulting in the "Disruptive civil technologies: six technologies with potential impacts on US interests out to 2025" conference report.

CALIFORNIA'S NEXT CENTURY 2.0

Why California? Because it is a vision of a world coming together and that concept is actually working in real life and not just a theory. "Leadership entails a sense of direction that mobilizes others."[7] The whole world needs to believe that we can all, from many different nations, still come together productively. California's existence is a reason to believe in this direction for the entire world's future.

Consider these two quotes from a discussion of whether the ancient Jews were a people:

"Our unity has been conserved in a different way, through forms different from those of all other peoples, but does this make us any the less a

---

[7] Zbigniew Brzesinski, *The Choice: Global Domination or Global Leadership* (Basic Books, 2004), 219.

people?"[8]

"Not because we are better than others, but because we have borne upon our shoulders and suffered all which calls for this. It is by paying the price for torments the likes of which the world has never known, that we have won the right to be the first in this work of creation."[9]

Historian Carey McWilliams wrote, "California is destined to occupy in the future, not a marginal, but a central position in world affairs...once the impact of this development really begins to make itself felt, California will come to occupy a new position in

---

[8] Anthony D. Smith, *Chosen Peoples: sacred sources of national identity* (Oxford university Press, 2003), 85.

[9] Ibid., 91.

the western scheme of things; not that of the
Colossus on the West, the Big Bully, the Untamed
Panther but the state which will link western
America with the Orient."[10]

CALIFORNIA COULD UNDERGO THIS BIG CHANGE:

- California is the land of trying something new and of innovation in the face of challenges. It has a very long and modern history of engaging in long-term, visionary, radical-change plans—and pulling them off with long-term commitment and dedication and hard work. Bans on smoking, use of seatbelts, sexual revolution, sensitivity to

---

[10] Carey McWilliams, *California: The Great Exception* (UC Press, 1940), 365.

gay people, multicultural sensitivity, voter initiatives, breast cancer awareness, climate change—these are all examples of mass change that occurred both at the government level and the mass society level as a part of an organized campaign for change.

- California has an extensive history in studying and pioneering practices in bringing understanding between different peoples and developing training for this. For example:
  - o The first ethnic studies department at a university where it would receive professional academic support was in California at San Francisco State University.

o The first universities to require diversity awareness training to graduate were at Stanford University and the California State University at Fullerton in California.

o The first interracial encounter group, named "Racial Confrontation as Transcendental Experience," occurred at the Esalen group in California. Encounter groups started the movement to diversity awareness training.

o The Human Potential Movement, a blending of Western and Eastern philosophies in order to achieve the deepest understanding of oneself, was also developed by the Esalen Institution founded in California. This psychological improvement program was so impressive that it was the first joint Soviet-USA scientific community, and it started the Soviet-American exchange program.

So California is, as its culture, well set to focus on how to bring different peoples together. In fact, "...historian Kevin Starr, who has written seven volumes about the state, has described California as an open-ended experiment in 'global ecumenical civilization.'"[11]

---

[11] Daniel B. Wood, "California, Once a Dream State, Strives to Get Back Its Groove," *Christian Science Monitor*, February 23, 2009.

- **"California is already at the leading edge of all of America in the future trends of where the global economy is going, by a significant margin over all other American states, and America itself combined,"** according to a report sponsored by the PPIC of the California state government in the most extensive look at California's global economic fit.[12] Compared to average states in America, California excels in a few areas—key to the particular characteristics of the emerging global trade network. Its investment in foreign businesses in "nonmanufacturing industries" and "manufacturing industries that use production-sharing" and its overall investment particularly

---

[12] Howard Shatz, *Business without Borders? Assessing the Globalization of the California Economy* (California PPIC, 2003).

in businesses in Asia (the world's largest future market) is significantly higher than all other US states. Foreign investment in total dollars was highest in California than any other state in America, as was total employees hired by a foreign firm. California's percent of exports to foreign countries was higher for the areas of "wholesale trade; information industries; professional, scientific, and technical services" including "publishing, motion picture and sound recording, broadcasting and telecommunications, and information services and data processing." California also exports a significantly higher amount of its total manufactured products than does the rest of America. Also, California's exports are more based on high-technology goods like electronic products and computers than the rest of America. More of the exports from California travel by air than by ship or land for the rest of America; more of the goods travel to Asia than the rest of America; and more goods from Asia come through California than any other American state. This creates a nuanced view of California's role to international business.

●

The PPIC goes on to say in the report that, "Although California's level of globalization is low on some measures, it is quite high on other measures. What characterized the globalization of the California economy is that in those parts of its economy where California is most international, it is at the leading edge of trends in globalization. The world is moving toward more production-sharing—the division of production processes among different countries. California is already there, with its outward FDI in Asia, its vast goods exports in the computer industries, and its provision of air-trade services for companies that depend on timely deliveries of inputs. The world is moving toward greater trade in services. California is already there, with its high level of services exports. Goods are increasingly moved by airplane rather than ship, in part because of the nature of goods being traded and in part because of changes in production processes. California port services exemplify this trend, with two-thirds to three-quarters of the value of all goods traded through the customs district of San Francisco transported by air. Finally, Asia remains the fastest growing world region economically, and California's Asia business links are far more extensive than those of the rest of the United States."

In *Global California: Rising to the Cosmopolitan Challenge*, Abraham Lowenthal points out that, "More than any other state's, California's economy is broadly and deeply affected by international trends..." and that "California is, in turn, the largest arena for foreign direct investment in the United States...twice as much as...New York."[13]

---

[13] Abraham Lowenthal, *Global California: Rising to the Cosmopolitan Challenge* (Stanford University Press, 2009), 9.

- Big problems in California will only enact this inherent ability to launch whole society change—the size of the problems in California is an opportunity because it will force change. "The opportunity to change," as it is called by change agents and Michael E. Porter (the Adam Smith of this era) in his book *The Competitive Advantage of Nations*, can't let status quo powers retain the old system, making it where the system must change. This event is an opportunity because most places never want to change. Change is scary and difficult and it is not normal for people from any culture to like change. Californians have a history of routinely radical change, and they **currently know they need to change, again, their whole system of government as explained in this book.**

CALIFORNIA'S NEXT CENTURY 2.0

California Choices is an academic union of scholars at UCSD, Stanford, UC Berkeley, and Sacramento State aimed at focusing on and finding solutions to California's "deep problems." California Forward is a grassroots organization with a larger base with the same goal. This is not routine complaining. California seems to have reached the concept only recently that they need not small but dramatic and massive changes to the entire system to simply survive. According to Daniel B. Wood, "Californians are finally sick of all this. There's never been such conversational currency with the intricacies of government by the average citizen."[14] In a 2010 issue of *Time*, Kevin

---

[14] Daniel B. Wood, "California, Once a Dream State, Strives to Get Back Its Groove," *Christian Science Monitor*, February 23, 2009.

O'Leary seconds this opinion, pointing out that

the people of California have finally woken up

that the system itself needs a complete overhaul:

"...Schwarzenegger was an 'illustrative

failure'...in trying to work within the existing

system to move the state ahead..." O'Leary

continues, "He did us a great service because he

tried everything. He fought with people, he

circumvented the legislature and went to the

ballot measure, he compromised, he tried for

spending caps, rainy day funds, raising taxes,

cutting programs, working with Republicans,

working with the Democrats."[15] Because

Schwarzenegger was "flexible and nothing

worked," the article concludes "...the governor

[15] Kevin O'Leary, "Hasta La Vista, Arnold: What is Schwarzenegger's Legacy," *Time*, November 1, 2010.

opened people's minds to the need for systemic

reform." Finally, released that same year, two

senior journalists, Joe Mathews and Mark Paul,

presented a series of bold, new, and sweeping

changes that would overhaul the entire

California government.[16] On top of this effort, a

joint partnership between Calit2 and CITRIS

created the report "California Dreaming:

Imagining New Futures for the State" that looks

at four entirely different visionary paths the

state could follow to grow into the future years.

- California was created by the Spanish in 1550

  (seventy years before the Pilgrims landed in

  Plymouth) specifically for the purpose of being

---

[16] Joe Mathews and Mark Paul, California Crackup: How Reform Broke the Golden State and How We Can Fix It, (UC Press, 2010).

CALIFORNIA'S NEXT CENTURY 2.0

an international trade port full of skilled workers literally from around the world. Immigrants trained as skilled laborers from Africa, China, and the Philippines, worked with Mexicans, El Salvadorans, and many native tribes, as well as Jewish and multiple European immigrants to provide logistics supports for trade between China, the Philippines, Japan, Mexico, and Spain. The Spanish built forts in order to secure the ports in the Bay Area, San Diego, Los Angeles, and further north. Over time these "missions" became settlements and led to the settlement of the rest of the state. So the entire history of California as a place centers on being an international trading post and bringing different goods and laborers from around the world in a mass production machine.

Natural ocean and air currents between California, Mexico, the Philippines, and Japan, naturally connecting Asia and Latin America and flowing right past the length of California state.

- Despite popular reporting, as mentioned above, California has a very effective government— one of the most effective in all of America and in the entire world. It's one of the most professional class of government bureaucrats, one of the most transparent, least corrupt, and closest to direct democracy in world.

CALIFORNIA'S NEXT CENTURY 2.0

- As already stated, California has a strong enough economy to survive on its own. Furthermore (despite popular reporting again) California has learned from its financial troubles and is on the way to being reformed in the needed political and institutional areas. Also, despite popular reporting, California is the worst hit state economically during this recession because of many things outside of its control— Enron caused a deficit in California, which being followed immediately by the global recession plunged California into a deep recession. But if California was not in debt before the recession, it could have surfed over the waves of the recession. Most states carry deficits for about ten years as they move to balance their budget; California did this right when the global recession of once every century happened.

Most states of almost all nations on Earth that are the main gateway for goods and people to that nation receive appropriate defense funding and infrastructure funding; California has nearly had to pay for the entire bill herself. California, despite sending as many troops to the war on terror as the highest rate of any state in America (Texas), has suffered most from the loss of America's world opinion directly to its economy. All of this happened while California was still taxed about seventy billion dollars by the federal government for services it never received, in what was called "Donor state welfare payments". California wasn't even

given a reprieve of being milked this $70 Billion
dollar tax (during its lowest economic point in
the last century) and literally received no
financial help at all from the federal
government. Without these multiple different
external events outside of California's control, it
still could have spent foolishly and survived this
current global recession. But all of the factors
listed above, at once, were too much for
California—and literally no other nation on
Earth could have withstood them—so the fact
that California is still intact is proof that it is
potentially stronger than any other economy in
the world. "In 2008, [during the height of the
recession] California's wipeout economy
attracted more venture capital than the rest of

the nation combined."[17]

- California is only missing the Brazilian community but already has as strong Brazilian presence that it can hold as a platform for expansion. The creation of a Brazilian community in California will start from a pre-existing base, making it very easy to grow.

- California has blue-ribbon commissions conducted on a range of topics and active within the recent past. Whatever the subject, the reports are always done by experts and received well.

---

[17] Michael Grunwald, "Why California Is Still America's Future," Time.com, October 23, 2009.

CALIFORNIA'S NEXT CENTURY 2.0

- California is an island separated by the largest ocean in the world to the west, a distance of uninhabitable desert that is equal in size from America to the Hawaiian Islands to the east, thick, unpopulated forest to the north, and a giant desert nearly the distance between California and MAP to the south. It is in essence a large urban population surrounded by unpopulated seas. This means that it has and will always have a unique, separate identity because of its physical separateness just as much as the islands of England and Japan that are technically closer to their neighboring population areas. As pointed out by author Peter Ahrens, in his website "the Next California"; "California is a vast landscape that contains virtually every type of natural feature, and it is relatively isolated from the rest of

North America and the United States by these

features, surrounded as it is by mountains,

desert, and ocean."

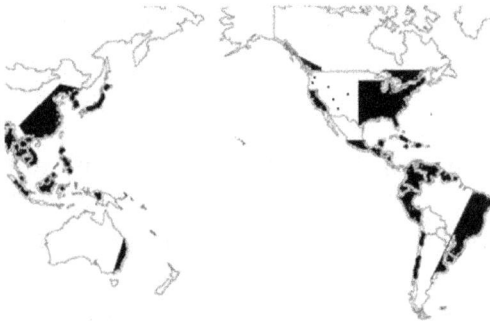

Black = populated areas

White = largely unpopulated

- Hong Kong and Scotland are both countries

  well-known to all Californians and both are seen

  as responsible and sound capitalist economies.

  Many Hong Kong people live in California, and

CALIFORNIA'S NEXT CENTURY 2.0

California has a strong Scottish community with regular Highlander events and an official California tartan that is unique to all of the tartans of Scotland. It will be easy for the idea of how these two countries are governed to be discussed at the mass level in California.

- This idea or any idea similar has never been tried before. There is no one who could definitively say that this won't work. The idea will have to be debated and will receive an attentive audience simply because it is truly new.

- This is literally the exact same argument that the "founding fathers of America" used to create America. All Americans are already familiar

314

with the main argument that is presented in this book. A government far away (the distance from London to Washington, DC, is nearly equal to the distance from Sacramento to Washington, DC) wants to extract as much money from a colony population as it can. The people from this colony (America) originally came from the homeland (England), but over time, because of mixing with vastly different cultures in large amounts (Natives, French, Dutch, Africans) in the area and dealing with different issues (having to work your own land and being able to own your own land), they began to feel that they were a different people—similar, but significantly different from the home population. The extraction of money from the colonies to England made the colonies much poorer than they otherwise would have been and went to fund a better life in an area far away that most colonists would never even visit. The English government said that the home government needed it and, besides, the colony was started by England and the colonists can't complain because they are represented fairly in the government of London by fellow English-cultured people who have their best interests in mind.

The colonists rejected this argument. They said that too much money was being taken, representatives in London were way too far away to be able to travel routinely to America to know what it was like, and that America was not fairly represented by politicians in London.

Rather, the colonists believed, London wanted to milk America for everything that it could and cared little for the life of the people in America—simply because it was so far away. "Had it not been for the fact that the effective social power is inversely proportionate to the distance from its centre, the American colonists would hardly have begun to cultivate the idea that taxes with representation are more enjoyable than taxes without representation."[18]

- If the thesis of this book is correct, the world needs a new negotiation center, and if it does not have it, then the world will recede into war and less economic growth. Furthermore, if the

---

[18] Leopold Kohr, *The Breakdown of Nations* (Chelsea Green Publishing Company, 1957), 65.

analysis of this book is correct, California is the only realistic option for being this new world nexus (i.e., if California does not endeavor to become this role, then it probably won't happen and the entire world will recede). While this sounds fantastic on the surface, the facts presented here attempt to show this is not a fantastic vision but a calculated probability. It takes twenty-five years for new ideas to catch on throughout a society. Most modern nations can't handle diversity now—and the diverse nations are horrible to minorities. Even if other nations tried to take on this role, it would likely take them three decades before they were in a position to even start, while California can begin today.

CALIFORNIA'S NEXT CENTURY 2.0

- The federal government has indirectly said that it needs California to start running itself as its own country. Environmental, insurance, and, previously, health care laws were allowed to be designed and fully implemented in California for the federal government while the government kept these powers for the other states in America. Also, California was the first government in the entire world to develop a plan for dealing with climate change as an official policy. California has a history of creating institutions that are of the same size and complexity as federal agencies focused on national issues. This, plus the fact that California created its own system of trade offices with foreign nations and has maintained them for decades, shows a proven ability to make new institutions to deal with global-level issues. Also, is the reality that creating international institutions is not as difficult as many people of the world might assume. New global institutions are being created all of the time, by many different nations. It is this ease of making foreign institutions that is helping to pull the world apart.[19]

- Also spurring from the point above, in economics there is a term called FIRE used to explain the main sectors considered most important in any domestic economy—finance, insurance and real estate. California already has independent control of insurance and

---

[19] Sebastian Mallaby, "Saving the World Bank," Foreign Affairs, May/June 2005.

independent control of environmental regulations—which dictate how homes and businesses can be built, a.k.a. how cheaply or expensively they must be built because of requirements in construction manners and materials. This means that California is already given by the federal government control over two of the three main drivers of every domestic economy. Furthermore, insurance is about 3% of the state economy, and real estate (renting and leasing property) is about 17% of the economy—meaning that California has a substantial amount of control to affect 20% of its economy already. The Great Depression of the 1930s was a 25% loss of the economy, almost causing total collapse. California is already allowed by the federal government to handle near the amount needed to cause total economic collapse in the state if it wanted to. That is proof of a good deal of trust by the federal government in the running of the state's economy. When added to the fact that it is against the basic nature of government agencies to parcel off work because it loosens their own power, the concept that the federal government did just this for California means that the burden of running California was more trouble than the additional power it brought to the federal government with its additional size. This is an inherently strong statement indicating the federal government feels California is too difficult for the federal government to govern.

Here's further proof: the federal government has publicly stated that it is "overwhelmed" with the demands of providing services for California. In 2008, years after the Katrina disaster, FEMA announced that it would not be able to handle a major disaster, the likes of which California routinely faces, such as earthquakes or wildfires.[20] That same year, the federal government admitted that it was "overwhelmed" by the number of Federal appeals cases in California.[21] Ten years earlier, the federal government admitted that it was "overwhelmed" by bankruptcy court proceedings in California alone—years before the current housing market

---

[20] "Report: Major Disaster Would 'Overwhelm' Aid groups," CNN, September 18, 2008.

[21] "Federal Appeals Court to Seek Five More Judges in Overwhelmed California District," How Appealing, 2008.

collapse and recession.[22] Even in the 1980s, when the president was from California, the federal government, months after a routine natural disaster, still could not handle basic responsibilities of a national government when it came to California.[23] Even the highest, most resourced court in all of America says that dealing with California's laws is too much: 42% of all federal Supreme Court cases come from looking into cases that California's Supreme Court, the highest federal court in California,

---

[22] Jason Booth, "Bankruptcy Court Overwhelmed," *Los Angeles Business Journal*, March 2, 1998.

[23] Miles Corwin, "US Hit on Quake Relief Role: Disaster: Watsonville Officials Assail Federal Emergency Management Agency. They Blame It for the 600 People Still Living in Parks, Shelters and Cars," *LA Times*, December 8, 1989.

started.[24] The Ninth Circuit is also currently the

largest of all federal court districts. The next

two largest circuit court areas in America have

only half the judges that the Ninth Circuit has.

The problem is so bad that two federal Supreme

Court justices testified in Congress that the

Ninth district was "too large" in 2007.

Also, and perhaps most important, is the fact

that the federal government has admitted that

California's economy is too large for the federal

government to provide the role that all national

governments provide to their states: that of the

financial backer and lender of last resort. During

the 2008 recession, California asked for a

---

[24] Debra Cassens Weiss, "9th Circuit Cases Make Up 'Staggering' Percentage of Supreme Court Docket," American Bar Association, October 5, 2011.

federal bailout. Experts admitted that California should receive the bailout because its economic downslide would greatly hurt America's economic recovery. But the secret came out: California is too big financially for the federal government to bailout, ever; even if the federal government wanted to, it's not large enough to support the subeconomy of California.[25]

- The only academic study of why nations are the shapes and sizes that they are (examining why an average nation state is roughly the size of France, Germany, Italy, Spain, Turkey, etc.)

---

[25] Declan McCullagh, "Is California Too Big To Fail?" CBS News, May 20, 2009; Ron Elving, "Why Obama Has to Bail Out California, But Won't," NPR, June 23, 2009.

says that California is large and strong enough to join the United Nations as a separate nation.[26]

(Also see Appendix III.)

AN INDEPENDENT CALIFORNIA ENACTING THIS GLOBAL PLAN IS NOT THAT RADICAL—EXAMPLES OF "SUBNATIONAL SOVEREIGNTY"

---

[26] Enrico Spolaore and Albert Alesina, *The Size of Nations* (MIT Press, 2005), 18.

CALIFORNIA'S NEXT CENTURY 2.0

SQUARE = past example

CIRCLE = current example

1900–2011

If California were to become its own nation in order to serve in the role as the new Switzerland for the next century, secession is an extreme way to achieve this status. Rather, there is another form of government that is best referred to casually as "secession-lite." Subnational sovereignty, where a nation has almost complete policy control except for the printing of money and the maintenance of national defense, is a rare form of government but one that has been practiced for over one hundred years. It is still practiced by a group of nations, almost all of which are very economically strong and politically stable. The term was coined by

CALIFORNIA'S NEXT CENTURY 2.0

Scotland, who is the newest recipient of this form of government, becoming "almost completely" independent four years ago after a full two hundred years as an official colony with all major decisions decided not in Scotland but London. Subnational sovereignty has been practiced by every region of the planet and with successful results. Statistically, this form of government has slightly expanded in the number of countries using its model. And it has also existed outside the modern world: for years the Roman Empire had a special relationship with Egypt, where it called Egypt its prefect; while grain continued to come to Rome from that state, Rome largely stayed out of all Egyptian affairs.

CALIFORNIA'S NEXT CENTURY 2.0

Past examples:

New Zealand, Australia, Canada, South Africa—

England

Finland, Ukraine—USSR

The Philippines—America

Lichtenstein—Switzerland

Bhutan—India

Current examples:

Macao, Hong Kong—China

Puerto Rico, Iraq—America

Iceland—Denmark

Quebec—Canada

Catalan—Spain

New Caledonia—France

Kurdistan—Iraq

Belarus—Russia

CALIFORNIA'S NEXT CENTURY 2.0

San Marino—Spain

Crete—Turkey

LEGAL PRECEDENCE—AMERICA HAS

ALREADY ALLOWED DIFFERENCES:

Specifically regarding sub-national sovereignty,

America has had numerous arrangements of this

sort of government already: the Philippines and

Cuba in the past operated to America as Scotland

does to England today. To a large extent, Iraq and

Afghanistan have this arrangement during their

transition to full sovereignty now. Also, post-war

Japan and Germany, during the brief period of less

than ten years where they were officially occupied,

could have no military except for US forces and

were issued currency by the American government

for use. Furthermore, America's recognition of

CALIFORNIA'S NEXT CENTURY 2.0

Kosovo as a separate republic from Bosnia set a precedent where a new state can separate from an existing state even if there is no known history for this separate state before.

This is also extremely close to the exact same deal that three different US presidents thought should be made available to Puerto Rico, leaving open a commission to help that nation choose its status in a free election since it was taken by force by the US military in the past. Currently, the Puerto Rican island is also going to have a vote to determine full or partial independence as proposed in the US Congress.

Also, while this situation would present a unique arrangement for California in comparison to the other states in America, the fact is that America has allowed unique rule sets for states and territories in the past and present. Eight states of the fifty, or almost one-fifth, have a unique legal environment that no other state in the entire union is allowed to have. Most of these eight have had this situation for over a century, and America has essentially accepted these unique situations:

- Texas was re-admitted to the Union separately by presidential decree, while all of the other Confederate states were claimed as never having left the Union. Furthermore, the Texas constitution says that it is not bound to the US president or US Congress, while all other state constitutions have to say this.

- Indiana was allowed to join the Union without having democratically ratified constitutions;

delegates just approved a constitution for the state, something no other state was allowed to do to join the Union.

- New Mexico has a legal requirement that all legal arrangements and court hearings must be in both Spanish and English, requiring bilingualism since the 1800s.

- Hawaii is both a state and a separate census category, meaning the federal government must keep track of the people of the state in the rest of the Union. No other state is allowed to have a separate census category (technically the Mormons of Utah have been a separate breeding population for hundreds of years just like Hawaii but would not be allowed to have a Utah census category).

- Louisiana is allowed to have a separate civil law, where marriages, inheritance, and divorces are different from legal requirements for all other states.

- New York state was allowed to declare in 1992 that they were exempt from the federal Tenth Amendment and could choose what federal laws under this amendment that it wanted to follow.

- Maine has, for almost a decade after 9/11, had a completely open border where people could walk across without identification all of the time. Only in the last two years have they had to undergo border security requirements like Washington, California, Arizona, New Mexico, and Texas.

- Finally, West Virginia skipped all of the requirements that every other state had to engage in order to become a state and was just declared a state by President Lincoln and is recognized as such.

There has never been 100% uniform application of federal laws to the states, nor has there been for the last one hundred years, and America did not suffer because of this allowance.

Additionally, the federal government has given three states the ability to make environmental law as binding as federal environmental law, giving these few states a federal power that forty-seven other states are not allowed to have.

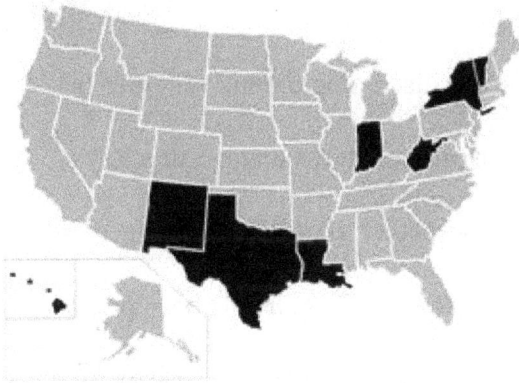

States that have been allowed by the Federal government (for decades to centuries) to behave in a way that no other state in the union is allowed to.

Furthermore, a discussion on this very idea has already been presented in a major national American newspaper: a call for an arrangement of this sort for California has already been proposed in the *New York Times*, in 2007, by Gar Alperovitz, a professor of political economy at the University of Maryland.[27]

Story 4: Besides the world needing this place, a world nexus, something beautiful could happen, the kind of beauty that only happens every four hundred years on Earth.

---

[27] Gar Alperovitz, "California as a Nation-State?" *New York Times*, February 12, 2007.

CALIFORNIA'S NEXT CENTURY 2.0

KNOWN RENAISSANCES IN THE LAST 5000 YEARS

Documented renaissance = circle

Possible renaissance = square

California is so diverse already, that if it becomes the world nexus for discussion, a unique global human cultural condition is very likely to occur—that of a cultural renaissance, the likes of which the world has only seen less than ten times in all of the known ten thousand years of human history. These explosions in science, art, commerce, philosophy, living standards, and overall evolution of the human mind have occurred throughout about .7% of the world's known cultures since the beginning of writing, and California, today in our era, could become one of them.

Past Renaissances

- Alhambra in southern Spain during the late reign of the Muslim Moors in Europe

- Byzantine Empire after the fall of Rome

- toward the end of the Byzantine Empire during the height of the Ottoman Muslim conquest of Europe

- Athens in Greece during the Greek golden age, 1000 - 700 BC

CALIFORNIA'S NEXT CENTURY 2.0

- Kushan Empire at Bagram in Afghanistan during the later half of the silk road era, 150–200 AD

- Baghdad in Iraq during the medieval period in Europe after the fall of Rome, shortly after the birth of Islam

- Ptolemaic Empire in Egypt, 305–30 BC, during the first half of the Roman Empire

- Timbuktu in Mali during 1300–1500 AD

- There is some evidence that there were renaissances in Hopewell culture in the Mississippi valley 100–500 AD

- Varangians Vikings in the Black Sea during the medieval ages

- A very limited-in-scope renaissance in southern France, 900–1000 AD, known as the Carolingian

- Tibet after the fall of the first Tibetan Empire and before the invasion of the Mongols

- Foijima Island in Japan during the European Renaissance period, around 1600 AD

- London during the height of the British Empire at the beginning of Second Industrial Revolution

- the most well-documented Renaissance in Florence, Italy, during the end of the medieval period in Europe.

With just the well-detailed renaissances in the last five thousand years of recorded human history or with the addition of the possible renaissances, the amount of cultures that will achieve a renaissance-level explosion of learning and art and innovation and beauty and science are about .5–6% of all known global cultures (according to some estimates). All of the renaissances had one main thing in common: a massive diversity far beyond whatever level of diversity any neighbors would ever have come into contact with that essentially channeled into a working world hub of manufacturing, product refinement, and distribution. A review of the conditions that all of the world's renaissances had indicates that California already meets most of the conditions for a spontaneous cultural eruption like the renaissances of the past and could easily meet the remaining conditions. Of the nineteen common characteristics of all global renaissances, California is only missing three characteristics and would need to improve on three that it already currently enacts (see Appendix II).

CALIFORNIA'S NEXT CENTURY 2.0

CONCLUSION:

The plan presented is such:

1. America frees the existing republics that were taken wrongfully and returns them to effective independence.

2. America embraces the new world market; it develops and partners itself with new American cultured nations who have UN and world body votes and expands its global Diaspora.

3. America pushes California to develop as the new global negotiation center for the new world order of new superpowers, and it continues its existing plans as it is working on them.

Together, these three additional policy pushes will overwhelm the globally negative trend against America to the point of reversing it so that America's presence returns to growth. Currently America is losing its global status and grip on influence—and the current plans for fixing the situation are not fixing it back to the way it was; they are at most only slowing the shrinking of the ring of influence. Consider that America is in the highest debt since WWII, has the worst public opinion across the planet since before WWII, and is in a world where there are equally powerful global powers with equal power to influence all of the corners of the world with the same political and financial influence that America wields today, since before WWII. Because of these facts, it seems imperative that America correct the trajectory of its global opinion immediately and that it consider these three additional steps as imperative to overwhelmingly and dramatically shift the global situation right now.

When considered with these weights, enacting the three radical steps seems the only rational option for America, especially when reviewing the current plans for fixing the situation—all of which do nothing more than repeat old strategies that enabled America's rise during the last, (and now obsolete) world order. Finally, the costs of these three proposals in consideration to their global impact is very small, only 15% loss of the American population and almost all of it from areas that most Americans never visit. The fact that the American nation will become more governmentally efficient and competitive in business and socially workable almost balances out the costs and makes this solution have (on the surface, when all things are considered) almost no net cost. Considering how fast the American population is growing, 15% loss of population will be temporary for only a very few years and then America would literally be right back to where it was.

America should make this change now while it is strong and the world would view the move as being able to see into the future. America would be perceived as having the willingness and courage to make moves with the assurance that it knows what it's doing and has the resources to handle any unforeseen issues. Doing this when the situation is bad will look like an act of desperation. Doing this now, when America is strong and appears on the surface to have many options (although it does not), will appear to the world as though America is a smart, shrewd, forward thinking, and courageous nation with drive and will—which will itself be another huge, globally expressed image boost.

As for California, it is hoped that this book will spur the public to discuss a million imaginative conversations. It is equally hoped the State government will conduct an official blue ribbon panel analyzing these proposals in detail to provide to the peoples' debate a solid foundation to rest upon.

CALIFORNIA CONSTITUTION ARTICLE 1 DECLARATION OF RIGHTS

SECTION 1. All people are by nature free and independent and have inalienable rights. Among these are enjoying and defending life and liberty, acquiring, possessing, and protecting property, and pursuing and obtaining safety, happiness, and privacy.

Appendixes

Arguments and concepts in this book are registered as intellectual property by the United States Federal Copyrights Office under two different titles:

Califia (TXu001312759 / 2006-07-21) and *California Deserves a Federal Bailout* (TXu001644750 / 2009-07-30)

Appendix I

Why California and America would want this new arrangement: They are not the same people, and forcing them to act like it hurts both socially and financially.

CALIFORNIA'S NEXT CENTURY 2.0

California and MAP are not the same people. There are many social indices, legal firsts, and demographics indicating a strong difference:

A. America does not have a fraction of the diverse population that California has as an entire state. Diversity on the level of California only happens in Seattle and New York City, maybe downtown Austin, Texas. For the rest of the states, it's roughly like the foreign trade percentage: about 5% diversity for most American states and 60% diversity for California. That's a gigantic gap, so big that other states just don't understand (at all by leaps) what California is going through. Yet Congress feels that it can make laws for California, although they are gigantically different as people. Would it make sense for

Uzbekistan to make policy for Afghanistan
because Uzbekistan has a good amount of
Uzbeks in Afghanistan, or for Saudi Arabia
to make policy for Iraq because Iraq has a
lot of Sunnis from Saudi Arabia? Haiti and
the Dominican Republic share the same
island and have some similar peoples but are
two different governments because they are
culturally two very different people. The
same is true for Singapore and Indonesia,
and Indonesia and East Timor. The
difference is people not from these regions
would assume, because they are somewhat
close by each other geographically, that they
are fundamentally the same people. Their
demographic background is substantially
different, and this makes (even if connected

by proximity) substantially different peoples.

B. America does not have the same politics as California—by a large margin. Desegregation, recognition of the Jewish holocaust survivors needing compensation, climate change, universal health care, gay rights, affirmative action, and the repeal of affirmative action, and on and on— California enacts radical laws about twenty to thirty years (on average) before the rest of America enacts those laws. That's the difference between Europe and the Middle East in terms of transmission of social concepts!

CALIFORNIA'S NEXT CENTURY 2.0

Here is a short list of things that California started twenty to thirty years on average before America (the *full* list would be pages long):

- Desegregation: 1930
- Banning laws against mixed-race couples: 1950s
- Gay rights: 1970s
- Repeal of affirmative action: 1990
- First gay social group: 1940
- Started environmental movement— Sierra Club
- First electric transit system for an urban area 1870
- Regional trademark product marketed to global customers— California Orange: 1880

- First mass labor fair practices strike—Chinese railroad workers 1867

- First union to maintain fair wages for trade workers—International Seaman: Seaman's Protective Association 1875

- Oil industry developed—Union Incotone Company, Central Valley: 1865

- First teachers' university—Normal School, San Jose 1862

- First ethnological survey—Stephen Powers, Tribes of California: 1877

- Health medicine industry: 1870

CALIFORNIA'S NEXT CENTURY 2.0

During the height of the 1960s' "counterculture" revolution, the way of breaking out of social modes was done very differently in California than the rest of America. Ken Kesey and the Magic Bus and the Band of Merry Pranksters were half of the hippie movement. They were primarily interested in fun, had no leaders or authors or key speakers, just free love in an open community with more and less active members. At this same time, the other half of the hippie movement was in New York, focused around Jack Kerouac, Allen Ginsberg, and Timothy Leary, who were clinical, controlled, academic researchers. These two groups were so different that when the California hippies traveled all the way from California to New York, the leaders of the East Coast movement did not like the Band of Merry Pranksters when they meet them, and Timothy Leary even refused to meet them.

And the differences in social opinion and social organizations don't stop in the past. For example in 1996 California eliminated affirmative action because the state had a high level of diversity inherently. Ten years later in 2003 and 2006, University of Michigan attempted to repeal affirmative action. In 2008 the state of Nebraska did this as did the state of Arizona in 2010. In Michigan and Arizona, 25% of the population was minority, and it's 7% in

Nebraska, whereas in California it is 60%.
States with a fraction of the minority
population of California have announced
that they too don't need to worry about
diversity.

During the debate for America to invade
Iraq in 2005, 70% of Californians were
against the war at the moment 70% of
Americans were in favor of the war (author
recalls). They held the exact opposite
opinions on a major national issue. More
recent proof: The federal government has
given California has its own insurance
regulation, environmental regulation, and
previously, health care regulation while
these same things are controlled directly by

the federal government for the rest of the states. The federal government has already recognized California as too complicated and "different" to manage, so they volunteered to get rid of these responsibilities for California and instead have the state handle them.

These are all small examples to supplement that every American and every Californian has heard this sort of talk for the last couple of decades on television, popular print journalism, and now routinely on Internet blogs. Michael Grunwald, on Time.com, wrote, "The media portray California as a noir fantasyland of overcrowded schools, perpetual droughts, celebrity breakdowns, illegal immigration, hellish congestion and general malaise, captured in headlines like 'Meltdown on the Ocean' and 'California's wipeout economy' and 'Will California become America's first failed state?' ...the crazy California criticism is likely to continue regardless of the facts...”[1]

There is also more hard scientific proof based on geography.

[1] Michael Grunwald, "Why California Is Still America's Future," *Time,* October 3, 2009.

CALIFORNIA'S NEXT CENTURY 2.0

Map of nations and their populations (European Union, Russia, China, India, Brazil, America)

Black = actual populated part of nation

Shaded = rest of boundaries of nation that are essentially unpopulated

The above population density map of the world best shows the population areas of the major superpowers, how they don't live in all of their claimed land (except Indian and Europe), how the overwhelming majority of the population of all of the superpowers is clustered together in one area with large gaps of land where there is basically no population (equal to the population of the Sahara Desert or the Brazilian rainforest). It also shows how sometimes there is another larger population within that superpower's boundaries but separated from the main population by a great distance. Other maps that show the same thing are world at night, and world emissions. The map above proves the concept of MAP (Main American population), where within the fifty states the overwhelming majority of all Americans live.

Almost half of America is not populated. MAP is located roughly from the I-35 freeway, almost literally in the middle of the country, straight north and south and then to the East Coast. This leaves all populated areas not within this area as American population islands (API). An American population density map (as well as maps showing all of America) will show: the interstate freeway system, farmland use, annual rainfall, county map, population change, most common industry, rural population loss, occurrence of ghost towns, detailed local roads, US congressional districts, and metropolitan planning districts. All will show a much greater level of detail on the right side of the map, almost from dead center all the way from north to south, than from the left side. The federal government is very aware of this giant population gap, issuing multiple reports[2] on the subject and issuing a new homestead act to try to repopulate the area.[3] However given the amount of money given by this plan to a city to actually repopulate it, the amount of money needed to repopulate the entire

---

[2] John B. Cromartie, "Population Loss Counties Lack Natural Amenities and Metro Proximity," ers.usda.gov; David A. McGranahan and Calvin L. Beale, "Understanding Rural Population Loss," ers.usda.gov.

[3] Howard Berkes, "The New Homestead Act: New Bill Aims to Repopulate Dying Towns Across the Great Plains," NPR, July 27, 2003.

gap between MAP and California is somewhere around $330 billion.

And regardless, there is evidence that this stretch of land is always going to be largely unpopulated. According to "Changing Patterns in US County Population: 2007 Annual Update" by Proximity (proximityone.com), the gap between MAP and California has existed since the 1940s. Also, a search for American ghost towns on the Internet will show that most are overwhelmingly within this gap area. A book written in 1981 called *The Nine Nations of North America* by Joel Garreau designates the space between California and MAP as the "Empty Quarter." This trend has also been reported on independently by academics.[4]

The peoples of MAP and California have a giant gap and therefore are not connected as a people.

The 2000 US Census observed, "Perhaps the most startling case is California, whose moderate net outmigration rate contrasted with high rates of net immigration in the neighboring states of Nevada and Arizona."[5]

---

[4] John C. Allen, "Center for Applied Rural Innovation"; "Chuck Hassebrook of the Center for Rural Affairs on the US Crisis in Family Farming," CNN, 2000; Edward McLean and Sara Newton, "US Counties and Equivalents, Inhabitant decline: 1990–2000," 2001.

[5] *Domestic Migration Across Regions, Divisions, and States: 1995 to 2000* (US Census 2000, Special Reports, 2003).

CALIFORNIA'S NEXT CENTURY 2.0

The same census showed most people who move outside of their state travel only to a nearby state; given that there is a great gap between the giant population of America and California, this means few people in MAP will ever immigrate to California.[6] This is backed up by census data that shows that there is a .5 coefficient greater chance that someone will travel from one state in MAP than they will move to California.[7] Statistically this is a significant amount. This pattern for less preference for California is also shown in airline prices, as the amount of trips between two areas sets the price for airline travel, not the physical distance. So the fact that airline prices are high between LA

---

[6] *State-to-State Migration Flows: 1995 to 2000* (US Census 2000, Special Reports, 2003).

[7] *State of Residence in 2000 by State of Birth 2000* (US Census 2000, Special Tabulation, 2005).

and New York City shows that people don't travel between California and the East Coast as much to other locations in MAP.[8] This pattern of a preference of Americans from MAP to travel to other MAP states but not to California is perhaps shown best in the interactive "American Migration" map provided by Forbes.com.[9]

This disconnect is not unique between MAP and California. It exists all over the world in areas where populations are separated by an equally large distance. The world essentially proves that

---

[8] Melonyce McAfee, "How Airlines Set Ticket Prices." Slate.com, November 22, 2006.

[9] John Bruner, "American Migration," Forbes.com, February 24, 2012.

CALIFORNIA'S NEXT CENTURY 2.0

**the dynamic of difference between MAP and
California is essentially a natural occurrence.**

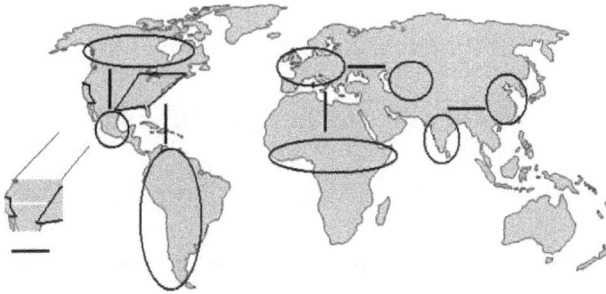

Circle = cultural region

Line = distance between California population and

MAP

Examples of areas of the world where there is an

equally large gap in population between two very

different established cultures are: Europe and

central Africa, Europe and central Asia, India and

China, North and South America, Mexico and
Canada, and America and South America.

**The above is not an anecdotal observation; it is
to prove that Americans and Californians see
each other as different and are different. This is
key because there is evidence that people who
are distant from each other are not only not the
same people, they also do not see each other as
the same inherently. Therefore they are more
likely to be hostile and take advantage of and
distrust each other, all of which can have serious
business and financial consequences.**

**New science seems to prove what people have
long suspected: that people who are physically
very distant from each other are also culturally**

very different from each other. They also have

very different views, ways of living, and opinions.[10]

Also, the theory of geographical determinism

discusses in general that geography primarily

determines the way people are and how they are

---

[10] Paola Giuliano, Antonio Spilimbergo, Giovanni Tonon, "Genetic, Cultural and Geographical Distances," 2006; Gary M. Olson and Judith S. Olson, "Distance Matters"; Philip J. Ethington, "The Intellectual Construction of 'Social Distance': Toward a Recovery of Georg Simmel's Social Geometry," 1995; Georg Simmel, *The Stranger* (1908); Anssi Paasi, "The Institutionalization of Regions: A Theoretical Framework," *Fennia* 164:1 (1986): 105–146; Anssi Paasi, "Deconstructing Regions: Notes on the Scales of Spatial Life," *Environment and Planning* A 23 (1991): 239–256; Allan Pred, "Structuration and Place: On the Becoming of Sense of Place and Structure of Feeling," *Journal for the Theory of Social Behavior* 13 (1983): 45–68; Allan Pred, "Place as Historically Contingent Process: Structuration and the Timegeography of Becoming Places," *Annals of the Association of American Geographers* 72:2 (1984): 279–97; Sumita Raghuram, Raghu Garud, and Batia M. Wiesenfeld, "Telework: Managing Distances in a Connected World"; Gunnar Olsson, "Distance and Human Interaction: A Review and Bibliography," 1965; A. Sen and T. E. Smith, "Gravity Models of Spatial Interaction Behavior," 1995.

different from other cultural regions.

And if two peoples are not in physical contact with each other, but are separated by a sea, giant mountain range, or inhabitable land, the same cultural distance occurs.[11]

Moreover, people far distant from each other see each other as different and think about each other as different from people they are physically close to. According to Marlone D. Henderson et al, "Unlike temporal distance, spatial distance from objects and events has received little,

---

[11] Donatella Della Porta and Mario Dani Blackwell, *Social Movements: An Introduction* (Publishers, 1999), 247–248, 274; Jim Taylor, Howard Means, and Watts Wacker, *The 500 Year Delta: What Happens After What Comes Next* (1997), 288; Enrico Spolaore and Albert Alesina, *The Size of Nations* (MIT Press, 2005), 19.

if any, attention in research on judgment and decision making."[12]

Taking it a step farther, there is also evidence that people at great distances from each other, not physically connected, tend to primarily use stereotypes to generalize about each other, rather than having an interest to learn facts about the people.[13]

---

[12] Marlone D. Henderson, Kentaro Fujita, Yaacov Trope, and Nira Liberman "Transcending the 'Here': The Effect of Spatial Distance on Social Judgment." Also see: Ran Kivetz and Yifat Kivetz, "Reconciling Mood Congruency and Mood Regulation: The Role of Psychological Distance"; Namin Shin, "Transactional Presence as a Critical Predictor of Success in Distance Learning," 2003.

[13] Yoav Bar-Anan and Nira Liberman, "The Association Between Psychological Distance and Construal Level: Evidence From an Implicit Association Test," (2006); E.

And there is evidence that the more you stereotype someone the more you are likely to be directly hostile to them or biased against them.[14]

This dynamic is supported by evidence that shows the more physically distant you see someone the more likely you are to take advantage of them, versus someone who you

---

Stephan, "Social Distance and Its Relation to Level of Construal, Temporal Distance and Physical Distance," Tel Aviv University (2006); Kentaro Fujita, Marlone D. Henderson, Juliana Eng, Yaacov Trope, and Nira Liberman, "Spatial Distance and Mental Construal of Social Events" (2006); W. P. Davison, "The Third-Person Effect in Communication," *Public Opinion Quarterly* 47 (1983): 1–15.

[14] M. D. Alicke, D. S. Vredenburg, M. Hiatt, and O. Govorun, "The Better Than Myself Effect," *Motivation and Emotion* 25 (2001): 7–22; M. D. Alicke, M. L. Klotz, D. L. Breitenbecher, T. J. Yurak, and D. S. Vredenburg, "Personal Contact, Individuation, and the Better-Than-Average Effect," *Journal of Personality and Social Psychology* 68 (1995): 804–825.

perceive as local.[15]

This aligns with research that shows that the further distance you are from a person the less trust you automatically have of that person.[16]

---

[15] Erin Bradner and Gloria Mark, "Why Distance Matters"; H. Tajfel, "Differentiation Between Social Groups: Studies in the Social Psychology of Intergroup Relations," 1978; B. Latané, "The Psychology of Social Impact," *American Psychologist*, 36(4) (1981): 343–356.

[16] B. V. Elsevier, "Trust and Trustworthyness," *Journal of Economic Behavior and Organization* (2004); Nancy Buchan, Rachel T. A. Croson, and Eric Johnson, "Trust and Reciprocity: An International Experiment"; Kambiz Heidarzadeh Hanzaee, "An Investigation About Exchange Behavioral Dimensions Impact on Industrial Buyer-Seller Relationships."

Evidence shows that without trust economic
interactions will be weak.[17]

American states in MAP are the same culture
because they are contiguous. This means that

---

[17] Brian Uzzi, "Embeddedness in the Making of Financial
Capital: How Social Relations and Networks Benefit Firms
Seeking Financing," 1999; Stephen Knack and Philip Keefer,
"Does Social Capital Have an Economic Payoff? A Cross
County Investigation," 1997; B. V. Elsevier, "Trust and
Trustworthyness," *Journal of Economic Behavior and
Organization* (2004); Nancy Buchan, Rachel T. A. Croson, and
Eric Johnson, "Trust and Reciprocity: An International
Experiment"; Kambiz Heidarzadeh Hanzaee, "An Investigation
About Exchange Behavioral Dimensions Impact on Industrial
Buyer-Seller Relationships"; L. Guiso, P. Sapienza, and L.
Zingales, "Cultural Biases in Economic Exchange" (NBER
Working Paper No. 11005, 2005); Alesina, Alberto, and Eliana
La Ferrara "Who Trusts Others?" *Journal of Public Economics*
85(2), (2002): 207–34; Jeffrey Frankel, Ernesto Stein, and
Shang-jin Wei, "Trading blocs and the Americas: The natural,
the Unnatural, and the Super-Natural," *The Journal of
Development Economics* 47 (1995): 61–95; Laura Bottazzi,
Marco Da Rin, and Thomas Hellmann, "The Importance of
Trust for Investment: Evidence from Venture Capital" (2006).

peoples who are not contiguous cannot claim the same relation.[18]

Ideas and culture travel easiest between peoples who are "close together geographically," which causes "direct diffusion through personal interaction emphasized by traditional literature."[19] In addition, "the concept of 'diffusion' has been imported into social science from physics, more exactly from studies of the diffusion of certain kinds of wave from one system to another."[20]

According to Jim Taylor et al, "Homophyly" is "the tendency of objects, when in close proximity, to

---

[18] Donatella Della Porta and Mario Dani Blackwell, *Social Movements: An Introduction* (Wiley Blackwell, 2006).

[19] Ibid., 247–248.

[20] Ibid., 274.

assume the characteristics of each other. Based on genetic theory, homophyly is equally applicable to human behavior."[21]

What's more, experts agree that "…individuals who are close together in space are also more alike in preferences…"[22]

The above has shown that Californians and Americans are culturally different from one another, see each other as such, and that research shows that people who view each other as distant and or different from one another will

---

[21] Jim Taylor, Howard Means, and Watts Wacker, *The 500 Year Delta: What Happens After What Comes Next* (Harper Business, 1997), 288.

[22] Enrico Spolaore and Albert Alesina, *The Size of Nations* (MIT Press, 2005), 19.

tend to take financial advantage of the other. As such, this third and final part of this appendix argument shows that, in fact, the consequences of the "distant" equals "different" social equation do result in net financial difficulties for California imposed upon it by the American culture.

This final section was saved for last because presenting it after the first two arguments have been made gives it weight and shows that it is actually happening just as presented here. Otherwise it might not have been accepted by the reader because of the acknowledged radicalness of what is said below.

CALIFORNIA'S NEXT CENTURY 2.0

A) Every year, California gives about one state
budget away in federal taxes, receiving nothing
in return. After California citizens' combined
federal taxes have paid for social security,
defense, commerce policing, and the normal
functions of the country, the leftover, extra
money never comes back to California.
Typically it fluctuates between seventy billion
dollars to near one hundred billion dollars.[23]

This money instead goes to pay for schools,
roads, police, and infrastructure for about two-

---

[23] *California Institute Special Report: California's Balance of
Payments with the Federal Treasury, Fiscal Years 1981–2003*
(The California Institute for Federal Policy Research); Pete
Shrag, *"What The Feds Owe Us, And What We Owe Ourselves*
(California Progress Report, 2009); Andrew Chamberlain,
"Why Do Some States Feast On Federal Spending, Not
Others," *Tax Foundation*, May 16, 2006.

CALIFORNIA'S NEXT CENTURY 2.0

thirds of the other states in America, who have
schools, roads, and policing that are rated near
the top of the fifty states in national reviews. At
the same time California is paying for thirty-five
states to live well, California routinely ranks
near the very bottom of the fifty states in
national reviews in every single category that it
gives money for thirty-five-plus other states to
do well in. California, according to the federal
government agencies who review standards, has
essentially the worst of everything. It has the
third worst roads in all fifty states.[24] School are
consistently rated worst in the nation.[25] It is not
a coincidence that California has the oldest

---

[24] "California Tops the List of Worst Roads in the Nation,"
Whittier Daily News, June 27, 2007.

[25] "California Schools Among Nation's Worst," *Los Angeles
Times,* January 4, 2005

school bus fleet in all of the fifty states.[26]

California's levees are as bad as New Orleans when Katrina hit.[27] The state with the highest rate of domestic and international air travel, California has the worst airports in the nation.[28] The situation is so bad that you can simply type "California worst in nation" in an Internet search engine and pages of articles, from official government studies, comes up.

This imbalance of federal taxes has existed since the late 1980s and has only grown in size.

---

[26] *Public Transportation Regional Agency Formation Study* (Fresno Council of Governments, 2007), 2–16.

[27] John Ritter, "Several Cities Are Dependent on Vulnerable Levees," *USA Today*, September 11, 2005.

[28] Shelby Grad, "LAX 'Worst Airport' Ranking Doesn't Surprise Officials," *Los Angeles Times*, May 16, 2009.

CALIFORNIA'S NEXT CENTURY 2.0

For nearly thirty years, California has paid for other states to continue to have a quality of life that is better than California's, and, as shown below in detail, there appears to be no sign this situation will ever change. For example, the federal government still asked for this tax imbalance even when California was the worst economically hit state in all fifty states during the current recession.

B) California is so big financially and at the opposite end of the bulk of the American population that it is always on the losing end of the federal government's national monetary policy. When financial times are bad, banks lower interest rates to release more loans so that more money flows into the economy, creating economic activity; when financial times are good, banks raise interest rates to cut back on loans, cutting down on the amount of economic activity in order to freeze or dramatically slow inflation. The goal of all economists in the world is growth with low inflation. Because of geography, and the gigantic size of America, California is always at a different place than the rest of the country. When America is coming out of recession, California is going into a big one; when America is in a recession, California is not part of it yet. This happened during this recession and the one during Bill Clinton's administration. Federal banks set monetary policy to help the majority of the country— which was the exact opposite of the monetary policy that California needs. This situation has

CALIFORNIA'S NEXT CENTURY 2.0

been known to the federal government since

FDR was president. While drafting new banking

legislation, FDR commissioned a study on how

to strengthen the dollar—the results were

interesting. FDR's economists suggested that a

separate West Coast monetary region be created

with a separate West Coast dollar. The reason

these economists suggested this in 1930 was to

prevent the exact situation that California faced

in 1990 and 2000.[29]

[29] Carl Walsh, "What Caused the 1990-1991 Recession," SF Federal Reserve; James Gerber, "Recession and Restructuring in the California Economy, 1990–1995," *Frontera Norte* 7, no. 14 (1995).

CALIFORNIA'S NEXT CENTURY 2.0

According to Jeffrey D. Sachs:

> During the decade from 1995 to
> 2005, then-Federal Reserve
> chairman Alan Greenspan over-
> reacted to several shocks to the
> economy. When financial
> turbulence hit in 1997 and
> 1998—the Asian crisis, the
> Russian ruble collapse and the
> failure of Long-Term Capital
> Management—the Fed increased
> liquidity and accidentally helped
> to set off the dot-com bubble.
> The Fed eased further in 1999 in
> anticipation of the Y2K computer
> threat, which of course proved to
> be a false alarm. When the Fed

subsequently tightened credit in

2000 and the dot-com bubble

burst, the Fed quickly turned

around and lowered interest rates

again. The liquidity expansion

was greatly amplified following

9/11, when the Fed put interest

rates down to 1 percent and

thereby helped to set off the

housing bubble, which has now

collapsed.[30]

This dynamic is further proved with an

exploration "Optimum currency area," a proven

---

[30] Jeffrey D. Sachs, "The Economic Need for Stable Policies, Not a Stimulus: An Exaggerated Swing Toward Economic Stimulus Will Only Delay The Return Of Sustainable Prosperity," *Scientific American* (2009).

concept of economics for half a century. Pioneered in 1961 by Robert Mundell, his "A Theory of Optimum Currency Areas" states that having one currency for the largest area possible and allowing a joint bank to have the greatest financial resources to help out any of its regions may not be the best idea because different regions may have different economic needs at different times. A slowdown in the economy in one region would require banks to lower interest rates and increase lending, but this would cause inflation to banks in another part of the currency area that have heavy economic activity—so a large bank may actually economically hurt its subregions. The theory was supported in 2001by Michael A. Kouparitsas, who said America does in fact have subregions that are not receiving their optimal currency treatment.[31] However, the theory goes back to the 1930s and FDR, whose advisors, when suggesting the first federal bank insurance plan, also studied the idea of subregional economic areas, recognizing the problems that Mundell would describe thirty years later (author's recollection). This concept has also been noted for the European monetary region, that perhaps a super-regional single currency isn't the best option and in fact is not based on pure economics but more on politics.[32]

---

[31] Michael A. Kouparitsas, "Is The United States An Optimum Currency Area? An Empirical Analysis Of Regional Business Cycles," Federal Reserve Bank of Chicago (2001). Also see: "Krugman, Mankiw, and the US as an OCA," Macro and Other Market Musings (2010); David Beckworth, "One Nation Under The Fed? The Asymmetric Effects Of US Monetary Policy and Its Implications for the United States as an Optimum Currency Area," *Journal of Macroeconomics* 32, no. 3 (2010).

[32] Kevin Dowd and Richard Timberlake Jr., eds., *Money and the Nation State—The Financial Revolution, Government, and*

CALIFORNIA'S NEXT CENTURY 2.0

Federal Reserve Districts

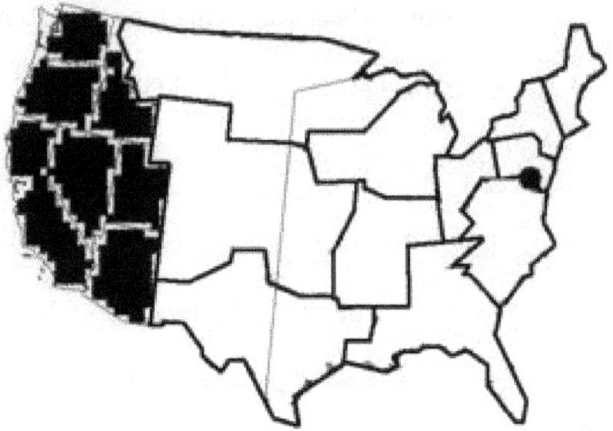

Shaded states = California's federal reserve district

Other shapes = federal reserve districts

Circle = headquarters for federal reserve system

In the above illustration, note that most of the

federal reserve sections, three-fourths of the

---

the World Monetary System, (Transaction publishers: 1998) 352, 357.

twelve, are within MAP alone. Also they are much smaller regions, meaning they get a lot more attention to develop economic analysis. They are all very close to the headquarters of the federal reserve where financial decisions are made. California is part of the largest single federal reserve district and is completely at the opposite end of the decision-making location in Washington, DC.

C) Originally California's 2000–2001 budget had a reserve of $1.78 billion.[33] Later on in 2000, the state was concerned it would it reach the SAL (state appropriations limit), a limit on the amount of money it could spend. It was afraid

[33] *Final Budget Summary: State Budget Highlights, 2000–01* (State of California).

that because it was going to take in more money than it originally estimated, by $4 billion, it would hit this policy ceiling for spending: "if current strong trends continue through the end of the year, revenues in 1999-00 will exceed the administration's January budget forecast by more than $4 billion."[34] CNN Money's Kit R. Roane reported, "in 2005, the California Legislative Analyst's Office (LAO) struggled with the issue, describing how a 20% upswing in annual revenues through fiscal 2000, turned into a 17% drop in 2002."[35]

---

[34] *Will California Hit the "GANN" Limit* (State Budget Project, April 2000).

[35] Kit R. Roane, "4 Reasons Why Texas Beats California in a Recession," CNN Money, July 13, 2010.

In 2001, the state was facing a twelve billion dollar budget deficit. California had to take out loans to cover this debt at much higher interest rates because it was not as good a credit risk due to its size and the fact it was already in debt. This dynamic caused the deficit to climb to thirty-five billion dollars by 2002, only a year later.[36]

From that time till 2012, the budget deficit for California was financially punishing, causing massive damage to the economy of California and placing it as the worst economy in all of America during this period. When the global recession occurred in 2008, California was

---

[36] John Broder, "Budget Deficit Climbs Steeply in California," *New York Times*, December 19, 2002.

already in massive debt and could not afford any economic stimulus programs for its economy, but it was left with the only option of allowing unchecked recession and massive cuts in government spending. If California was not in massive debt before the global recession of 2008, it never would have needed a bailout and would have been able to move through the recession in a strong position, possibly to the point of not being hurt economically at all. The proof: Texas, during the global recession, had a growing economy because the government was able to fund some stimulus programs. Texas entered the global recession with the economic surplus that California had in 2000 but lost by

CALIFORNIA'S NEXT CENTURY 2.0

2001.[37]

The Texas economy survived the recession in good shape, whereas the California economy became the worst in the nation. Texas too had a massive deficit in the past that it had to pay off, but it had already paid out this deficit before the global recession. As such, it was in a position to take out loans on good credit terms to continue to fund its economy through the global retraction of money in 2008 up until the present. *The Economist* explained, "In part this is because Texan banks, hard hit in the last

---

[37] Derek Thompson, "How Texas Is Dominating the Recession," *The Atlantic*, July 31, 2010.

property bust, did not over expand this time."[38] The source of California's status as worst economy in America during the global recession was caused because of the budget deficit that started in 2001. The question therefore is what happened in 2000 to 2001 to cause overspending by the state to the tune of more than ten billion dollars? California's Budget Project proposed that "California's energy crisis has overshadowed deliberations over the 2001-02 fiscal year. At issue are amounts spent by the state to purchase power for customers of the state's electric utility companies and concern over how the crisis will affect the California economy and, in turn, state revenues. In brief,

---

[38] "California v Texas: An Intriguing, Much More Equal Rivalry Out West. But Both California and Texas Can Learn from Each Other," *The Economist*, July 9, 2009.

wholesale price increases, supply shortages attributable to a number of factors, and elements of the state's deregulation law set the stage for the crisis."[39]

When California deregulated its energy market, which took effect in 2001, many companies based in Houston, Texas, deliberately raised energy prices to unreasonable levels and created or lied about a limit in production to justify the costs.[40] At this same time, Texas was the state that the president of the federal government at that

---

[39] *What Does California's Energy Crisis Mean for the Budget?* (California Budget Project, 2001).

[40] Christian Berthelsen and Mark Martin, "Feds Reveal 2 Enron Firms' Energy Scheme: 'Death Star' Tactic Manipulated Market," *San Francisco Chronicle*, November 23, 2002.

time came from, and Enron and many Houston-based energy companies were known to be close friends and longtime massive financial contributors George W. Bush for years before he ever became president.[41]

Four years later, a federal investigation judged that Enron and other Houston-based energy companies illegally price gouged the California economy, causing the budget surplus to turn into a deficit within one year. It took nearly three years for the federal government to even be willing to look into the case, during which time California's

[41] Frank Pellegrini, "Bush's Enron Problem," *Time*, January 10, 2002; Tim Wheeler, "Enron Put Bush in White House," *People's Weekly World Newspaper*, January 18, 2002.

deficit and the destruction to the California economy only dramatically increased. It is perhaps not a coincidence that during this time, the attorney general for the federal government was forced to remove himself from investigating Enron because he had received financial contributions from the organization in the past. It was not until 2003 that the Federal Energy Regulatory Commission finally concluded that price gouging had in fact happened.[42] As reported on NewsMax.com, "In a speech at UCLA on August 19, 2003, [California Governor Gray] Davis apologized for being slow to act during the energy crisis,

---

[42] "The Western Energy Crisis, the Enron Bankruptcy, and FERC's Response."
http://www.ferc.gov/industries/electric/indus-act/wec/chron/chronology.pdf

but then forcefully attacked the Houston-based energy suppliers: 'I inherited the energy deregulation scheme which put us all at the mercy of the big energy producers. We got no help from the Federal government. In fact, when I was fighting Enron and the other energy companies, these same companies were sitting down with Vice President Cheney to draft a national energy strategy.'"[43]

---

[43] Charles R. Smith, "Enron and Davis," NewsMax.com, August 22, 2003.

CALIFORNIA'S NEXT CENTURY 2.0

In the end, only Enron, and not the other companies who price gouged California, had to pay. Of the money that Enron stole from California through illegal means, it only was required to pay about one-tenth of the amount taken. Of that amount, California is only expecting to see about one-sixth, or around 3%, of the total amount taken from the California economy. Additionally, no money will have to go to pay for the interest on the loans California had to take out to cover its debt or for the general pain caused to all of California. Additionally, no penalties or punishment of any kind will happen to anyone in the federal government for waiting for years to even investigate a decision that

CALIFORNIA'S NEXT CENTURY 2.0

almost destroyed the entire state's economy.[44]

What is interesting is that none of this information about the federal government lack of action, and possible protection of wrongdoing, was brought up at all when California asked for a federal bailout in 2008.

D) For the first five years after 9/11, the majority of 9/11 homeland security funding went to Texas (the home state of the president at that time) to protect oil refinery ports. Federal government officials acknowledged at this time what everyone already knew: terrorists will attack the weakest points in the border system of

---

[44] "Enron Settles California Price-Gouging Claim," CBS News, July 15, 2005; Jonathan Peterson, "Enron Settles State Claim of Price Gouging," Los Angeles Times, July 16, 2005.

CALIFORNIA'S NEXT CENTURY 2.0

America—the seaports and airports—where millions of people and tons of good are moved through ports every day. The majority of goods into the country comes through the seaports in California. Only 2% of all cargo at this time was inspected. The death toll for an attack on a seaport in California or New York was estimated to be possible between ten thousand to one hundred thousand lives (if a radiological bomb or biochemical warhead was exploded). However, despite federal terrorism official warnings and pleas from California and New York, only a fraction of homeland terror prevention funding went to the actual most vulnerable targets in the US. The rest went for states in the Midwest to buy equipment that they would never even use—literally wasted money.

CALIFORNIA'S NEXT CENTURY 2.0

And a gigantic chunk of the money (at the same time that California and New York ports were unprotected) went to oil ports in the state of Texas. Only Diane Feinstein still complains about this—and California has yet to see the money or an apology for not being protected during a time of imminent danger. California and New York, the sites of all of the protests against the Iraq war, were given a small fraction of the money that they needed to protect the open seaports and airports that receive the majority of foreign goods and people entering the country. Texas, which is not a major foreign goods destination or travel destination, received more money then it knew how to handle, and the majority of funds for seaport security went to Texas ports that mostly ship oil. The potential loss of life of a Texas oil port compared to a

California goods seaport are different by factors

of multiplication. Right after the worst attack

against Americans since Pearl Harbor,

Californians' lives were put at needless risk of

massive death on a scale that would dwarf 9/11,

while money was wasted on parts of the country

that federal terror officials acknowledged had no

real terror threat.[45]

[45] ("Senators Feinstein and Cornyn Offer Measure That Would
Ensure That More Homeland Security Grants Are Based on
Risk," Feinstein Senate Website, 2007; Fred Lucas,
"Homeland Security Cash for Bingo, Limos," NewsMax.com,
2007; Veronique de Rugy, "What Does Homeland Security
Spending Buy?" American Enterprise Institute, 2004; "Bush
Administration Strikes Back Against Critics; No Smoking on
the Beach?" *Paula Zahn Now*, CNN News, 2004; Mimi Hall,
"Homeland Security Money Doesn't Match Terror Threat,"
USA Today, 2003; Joe Conason, "Politics As Usual Instead of
Security," *New York Observer*, 2006; "Editorial: An insecure
nation: Real Security, or Politics as Usual?" *New York Times*,

CALIFORNIA'S NEXT CENTURY 2.0

During this same time that 9/11 funding was diverted from the state that was the most vulnerable to terrorist attack, the official White House website posted a major national television figure, who publicly supported the existing president, saying that it would be okay if a terrorist attack blew up a major California city (discussed below). The trend is disturbing.

9/11 homeland security funding 2006

2005; Peter Dujardin, "Local Port Denied Security Funds," DailyPress.com, 2005.

CALIFORNIA'S NEXT CENTURY 2.0

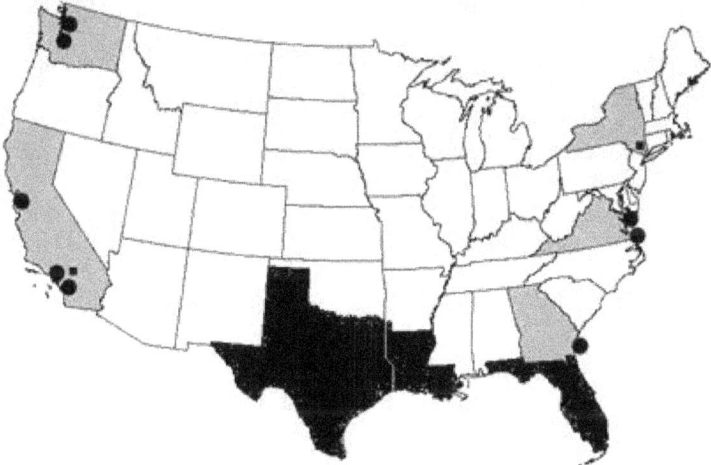

Circle = busiest seaport for international

destinations

Square = busiest airport for international

destinations

Filled in state = states receiving the most funding by

far for homeland security

None of the busiest sea- or airports, the major ways that anything from outside America can enter the country, were in the top three of homeland security funding. No sea or airport in Texas, Louisiana, or Florida even made the list as a major international destination.[46]

E) The whole point of federalism is to enact the benefits of a federation for the members. A group of states can pull funds and resources together to better provide for the member states—such as a greater defense force through a combined army or emergency funds if a state has a natural disaster or a major need. This was the reason for the first federal democracy in all

---

[46] Ronald D. White, "North America Ports Report Record Traffic," *Los Angeles Times*, February 4, 2006.

of human history—the Athenian Greeks, the Greenland Vikings—and later with the American states. America violates the spirit of federalism with its behavior toward California.

During the current recession, being the worst hit by the recession in all fifty states, California asked for a bailout from the federal government in order to stay economically afloat.[47] The state argued that it too was "too big to fail" and should be bailed out like the national banking businesses and

---

[47] Joshua Zumbrun, "Where Recession Will Hit Hardest," Forbes.com, 2008; Tom Royce, "Top 10 Worst Foreclosure Cities For 2008," The Real Estate Bloggers, 2009; Josh Zumbrun, "The Best and Worst Cities for Recession Recovery," Forbes.com, 2009; "Tent City in Sacramento CA Held Up as National Example," MSNBC; "Unemployment In June: The Worst-Hit Cities (MAP)" Huffington Post, 2009; John O'Connor, "Why Surrender a Home in Bankruptcy?" The National Bankruptcy Forum.

national automotive companies. The federal

government declined to give any financial aid to

California at all. The question for Californians

is, why did the automotive industry receive a

bailout, out of fear that it would hurt the US

economy, if it was allowed to collapse, yet

California wasn't? The automotive industry

supplies 4.7% of US jobs, and California

provides nearly three times that amount at 13%

of the national economy in the year of the

recession.[48] The federal government said that it

wasn't providing bailouts to states, yet all three

of the major automotive businesses that received

bailouts were located in the state of Michigan,

which effectively received a massive state

---

[48] Catherine Rampell, "How Many Jobs Depend on the Big Three?" *New York Times*, November 17, 2008.

economic surplus.[49] Furthermore, when the auto giants were receiving their stimulus, the area of the country that Michigan was in was already on its way out of the recession and showing significant signs of recovery when California was showing no signs.[50] The federal government was warned that letting California fall could stall economic recovery for the entire nation, so bailing out California was good for America.[51] It was also warned that letting government jobs close was no way to get out of

---

[49] Karen Travers, Matt Jaffe, and Thomas Giusto, "President Obama Hails Auto Industry Recovery in Michigan," *Los Angeles Times*, January 29, 2010.

[50] Armen Hareyan, "Pending Home Sales Up In a Sign of Recovery," Huliq, February 3, 2009; "Survey Shows Sluggish Midwest, Plains Economy," Seeking Alpha, September 1, 2011.

[51] Kevin O'Leary, "Can the US Afford to Let California Fail?" *Los Angeles Times*, June 19, 2009.

a recession in general.[52] Furthermore, California only asked for a bailout one-eighth the size of the amount given to the automotive industries (although they only supply one-third of the jobs of California's economy), and it was refused the bailout in 2008.[53] At this time California was the worst hit state in the nation for the recession and desperately needed help. No help came.

In 2012, four years later, California was still the worst hit state in all fifty for the recession, and America was still in an economic recession that did not improve as fast as the federal

---

[52] Annie Lowrey, "Don't Freeze Federal Pay. Cut It. Improving Obama's Wishy-Washy Plan to Hurt Some Workers Without Helping Others," Slate.com, 2010.

[53] James Joyner, "California May Need $7 Billion Bailout," Outside the Beltway, October 3, 2008.

government had hoped. Seven of the ten worst hit cities in all of America were in California alone.[54] California was not given a bailout because the federal government hypocritically said it was not bailing out states and only bailing out industries too large to fail. All this occurred despite the fact that California was not one of the average level of economically hurt states but the *most* hurt state in the Union.

This should not be a surprise because California has received the exact same response from the federal government for recessions in the past.

---

[54] "10 Worst Cities for Finding a Job," *US News & World Report*, January 20, 2012.

CALIFORNIA'S NEXT CENTURY 2.0

In the 2008 recession, California voted for Barack Obama and was overwhelmingly stocked in state political positions by people from the president's same party. In 1992, during the recession then, California again overwhelmingly voted for the president at that time and had people in political position in the state from the president's same party. At both times, California was the most hurt state in the nation, and at both times, California received no help from the federal government.[55] Even when completely politically aligned with Washington,

[55] Patrick Lee, "As Clinton Goes, So Goes the State : Economy: Recession-Weary California Stands to Benefit If the President-Elect Can Deliver on His Campaign Promises," *Los Angeles Times*, 1992; Patrick Lee, "State to Feel Full Effect of Changes: Economy: Clinton's Proposed Tax and Spending Plans Are Likely to Hurt Californians More Than Other Americans—But They May Help More Here Too," *Los Angeles Times*, 1993. *The California Economy* (Legislative Analyst's Office, January 1995).

DC, California has never received help during a recession for the last twenty years.

Despite being the worst hit state during the recession and receiving no help, California still had to pay about one full state budget in extra federal taxes for services that it never saw. And that went to help states primarily in the Midwest and South, who during this time were already on their way out of the recession.[56] A fraction of the federal tax dollars that are taken with no return services being provided

[56] Armen Hareyan, "Pending Home Sales Up In a Sign Of Recovery," Huliq, 2009; "Survey Shows Sluggish Midwest, Plains Economy," Seeking Alpha, 2011; *California Institute Special Report: California's Balance of Payments with the Federal Treasury, Fiscal Years 1981–2003* (The California Institute for Federal Policy Research); "State and Local Tax Burdens: All States, One Year, 1977–2009," Tax Foundation, 2011; ("Federal Taxes Paid vs. Federal Spending Received by State, 1981–2005," Tax Foundation, 2007.

during the recession would have moved California into economic stability, rather it was allowed to suffer the most and still had to pay to help others who were currently suffering less.

But the burden from the federal government while California was in its worst financial situation does not end here. Fire season is a major annual occurrence in California due to its proximity to the giant Sierra Nevada forest. Ever year California has to control forest fires that could do millions of dollars in damage. When California asked for help in controlling the forest fires in 2008, just like midwestern states ask for flood and tornado assistance, none was given by the federal government, from president George W. Bush to governor

Schwarzenegger, although both were from the same political party.[57] The degree of nonassistance was so bad that the governor stopped campaigning with the president.[58]

California, on its own financially, attempted to save some money with innovative policies but was stopped from implementing them from the federal government, costing California even more money.[59] Agriculture is one of California's main economy industries. The

---

[57] "Bush Vows Not to Leave California Stranded As Firefighting Costs Strain Budget," West Coast 911, July 18, 2008; Veronique de Turenne, "California Faces Its Fire Season Without Promised Cargo Planes," *Los Angeles Times*, 2008.

[58] Robert Salladay, "Schwarzenegger Deeps Distance from Bush Campaign," *Los Angeles Times*, 2004

[59] David Knowles, "Schwarzenegger: Ship Calif. Prisoners to Mexico," AOL News, January 26, 2010.

federal government imposed a harsh

interpretation of the Endangered Species Act

and demanded that California water not go to

crops but to save a small fish.[60] The situation

was so bad that the Governor Schwarzenegger

begged Washington to allow more water for

farms during this recession; he received no help

and instead was given a lecture by President

Obama that water is a privilege not a right.[61] At

this same time, 2009, the federal government

created a new policy that would raise hospital

---

[60] Steve Poizner, "California Water Shortage Exposes Big Government Run Amok," BigGovernment.com, 2010.

[61] "Schwarzenegger Seeks Aid For California Drought Zone," Norms Revenge, AFP on Yahoo, 2009; John Loudon, "Obama to California 'Water, Its [sic] Not a Right Its [sic] a Privilege,'" BigGovernment.com, 2010.

costs for California hospitals by 10%.[62] Also during this time, ten states with historically better education systems and better economic situations were given extra money for education funding while California received no money.[63] At the same time, although California ports deliver most of the foreign imported goods to all of America, the federal government said that it would provide no assistance to improve the ports and all of the money would have to come from California itself.[64] However, at this exact same period, the federal government gave six

---

[62] "A New Government-Run Plan Would Impose Significant Financial Losses on California Hospitals," PR Newswire, July 16, 2009.

[63] Howard Blume, "California Loses Bid for Federal Race to the Top Education Grant," Los Angeles Times, August 24, 2010.

[64] John O'Dell, "Clean Truck Program at So Cal Ports Is Becoming Victim of Success," AutoObserver.com, 2009.

hundred million dollars to help improve the port of New Orleans in Louisiana, a state not as hard hit from the recession for a port that delivers a fraction of the goods to America that California's ports do.[65]

Then the federal government threatened to take away millions of dollars from California because it was not spending the money fast enough.[66] Then, although protecting the borders if one of the main responsibilities of all national governments around the world, the federal government said it would provide no help for

---

[65] Jenny Jarvie, "The US Approves Mississippi's Plan to Divert $600 Million. Critics Say the Poor Are Being Shortchanged," *Los Angeles Times*, January 26, 2008.

[66] Paresh Dave, "California Officials Push Agencies to Spend Federal Stimulus Funds," McClatchy News, 2011.

illegal immigration to California, but instead it

would create new rules to make California's

enforcement of its borders cost even more.[67]

At the same time that the federal government

gave housing assistance to other states but none

to California it passed new regulations that

made home ownership more expensive in

California.[68]

The collective situation was so bad that

governor of California lashed out at the federal

---

[67] "Illegal Immigration Costs Everyone. So Why Is Washington Forcing Expensive New Rules on the State?" *Los Angeles Times*, 2008; "State Seeks More Federal Aid for Cost of Keeping Illegal Immigrants," CCPOA.org.

[68] Kevin Halifax, "HUD Left Out California, Nevada, Arizona & Florida—Why?" VelocityRealityGroup.com, 2011; Catherine Saillant, "Homeowners Forced to Buy Flood Insurance After FEMA Redraws Maps," *Los Angeles Times*, 2010.

government regarding what appeared to be direct abuse during the state's greatest time of need. "The federal government is part of our problem," said Schwarzenegger. "We are currently owed billions of dollars by the federal government for various programs. We no longer can ignore what is owed to us, or what we are forced to spend on federal mandates," he declared.[69]

It appears that California is never helped out by the federal government, no matter how bad the situation is, whether the political party running the federal government is the same one running the California government.

---

[69] "Schwarzenegger Calls Out Federal Government, Asks for Aid," Personal Liberty News Desk, January 12, 2010.

This situation has existed for literally decades. And even when California is most in need, the federal government, besides providing no assistance, will continue to take money from the state to pay for extra programs for others, apparently having no problem with making the California economy even worse. If the state and the national government were people, it certainly would be described as an abusive relationship. The following information provides indirect proof.

"Othering" is the term in sociology where a group uses a different group to define what they are by pointing out how they are different. It is also called "alterity," "out-group/in-group identification," "intersectionality," or "negative identity." In anthropology it is defined as "comparing ourselves to others and as the same time distancing ourselves from them." The effect on the "othered" group is defined as "differences used as a weapon of self-devaluation by internalizing stereotypical societal views, thus leading to a form of psychological oppression (in psychology this is known as self-fulfilling prophecy)." It is defined as when one group exaggerates some existing differences in order to construct from the ground a whole culture of who they are.[70]

<Begin Sidebar>

More Specifics on What Othering Looks Like

---

[70] Stephen Riggins, "The Rhetoric of Othering" in *The Language and Politics of Exclusion* (1997); Michael Taussig, *Mimesis and Alterity* (1993); Clive Hazell, *Alterity and Experience of the Other* (2009); Johannes Fabian, *Time and Other: How Anthropology Makes Its Object* (1983).

- "In this consciousness, nations, national identities and national homelands appear as 'natural.' Most crucially, the 'world of nations' is represented as 'natural,' moral order. This imaging of 'us,' 'them'."[71]

- "Stereotyping them."[72]

- "If the imagining of foreignness is an integral part of the theoretical consciousness of nationalism, then foreignness is not an undifferentiated sense of 'Otherness'."[73]

- "This analysis is based on the assumption first that collective identity is not naturally generated but socially constructed: ...the

---

[71] Michael Billig, *Banal Nationalism (Sage Publications, 1995)*, 10.

[72] Ibid., 78–83.

[73] Ibid., 80.

distinction of the other, is symbolically constructed and defined."[74]

- "According to Chambers (1997), others are those who are implicitly or explicitly evaluated with the standards set by the dominant group, while the nature of the dominant group remains unexamined"; "Finally, in the process of comparison and examination, the dominant group not only defines the other as separate and 'not us' but also places a value judgment upon the experiences of the other."[75]

---

[74] S. N. Eisenstadt, "Modernity and the Construction of Collective Identities," *International Journal of Comparative Sociology*: 39, Issue: 1 (1998).

[75] Charlotte Chorn Dunham, Julie Harms Cannon, and Bernadette Dietz, "Representing the *Other* in Sociology of the Family Texts," *Sage Journals*, 2004.

- "In short, 'we' gain our sense of self through opposition; we 'know' who we are because 'we're not like them.' And we justify our power over others through the process of othering."[76]

<End Sidebar>

These differences can be based on language, religions, diet, looks, or just the "out-group" living in a different area that's easily defined geographically (the ancient Greeks fought many fierce battles based on this concept—the legendary battle of Troy is the most famous). England used the Irish over hundreds of years to develop the concept of the proper English gentleman to the drunk angry

---

[76] James Jasinski, *Sourcebook on Rhetoric: Key Concepts in Contemporary Rhetorical Studies* (Sage Publications, 2001).

Irish. Other examples include: white Southerners to black slaves in the South, early American settlers to Native Americans, Japanese to the Ainu, Turkish to the Greek, Greeks to the Turkish, Nazis to the Jews of pre-WWII Germany, Mexicans to nonintegrated native peoples today, Russians to Chechens and the Vladivostok region today, Romanians to Gypsies, all of the EU to Muslims right now, and all of Europe as the Occidental region to all of Asia as the Oriental region for more than one hundred years in the 1800s. USA developed an understanding of American values in contrast to the Soviet Union for seventy years. Men and women defining who they are in contrast to each other was and enormously popular belief until the 1960s. Conservative and liberal political parties identify themselves directly based on being the opposite of the other party—and the two-party system has lasted the entire history of America.

Not surprisingly, examples commonly used are groups that have a strong presence in California but not in MAP in general (e.g., Jew, Muslim, gypsy, foreigner, or immigrant) are believed to have problematic and even highly negative, in some cases dangerous, characteristics. Those identified as "aliens" differ in their "threat" or "the dangers they pose": Gypsies, Jews, Muslims, Latin Americans.[77] This helps to explain why othering happens from America to California. Othering to California started in 1960s with the hippies, but this was literally two years after the Civil Rights Act was

[77] Tom R. Burns, Masoud Kamali, and Jens Rydgren, "The Social Construction of Xenophobia and Other-isms," 2001.

signed, marking a point where it was no longer okay to publicly criticize minority groups—the traditional group used to other to create an American identity. This is not a coincidence. **Regional discrimination to create a boundary identity replaced demographic discrimination. America uses California for the purpose of social cohesion of the main American population.**

How do we know that America uses California in the manner described? Here are the acts suggesting this:

Former President George W. Bush's long-time senior media advisor admitted that people in the Midwest, the main part of MAP, do not like people in the West Coast and don't read the *LA Times*.[78]

The vice president of the time, Dick Cheney, referred to all Californians by a slang term, saying that they were nothing but "Marin county hot-tubbers."[79]

Also half of the antiwar protests on February 15, 2003 (organized across the country against the invasion of Iraq) occurred just in California alone. California was the only state in the Union to protest the war, although other cities did. However, major national news agencies said that all the protestors were "un-American" and "un-patriotic," showing that a lot of the distrust about

---

[78] Ron Suskind, "Faith, Certainty and the Presidency of George W. Bush," New York Times, October 17, 2004.

[79] "Bush Sr. Apologizes for Marin Hot Tub Slam," Associated Press, February 28, 2002.

being proper Americans is aimed at California.[80]

Interviewed later on about California, a famous World War II bomber pilot said that he thinks are Californians aren't good Americans.[81]

In 2006, on the official White House website, the Reverend Jerry Falwell, who had been a campaign contributor for President Bush, said that it would be okay by God if terrorists blew up San Francisco.[82] Falwell has also made it clear that he thinks

---

[80] "Headline: Iraq War / Protest vs. Patriotism," *NBC Evening News*, April 18, 2003; Deborah Jaramillo, "Protesters and War: An Excerpt from Ugly War, Pretty Package: How CNN and Fox News Made the Invasion of Iraq High Concept," Huffington Post, 2009.

[81] "*Enola Gay* Navigator Thinks Californian's [sic] Aren't Patriotic," calguns.net.

[82] "Ask the White House: April 23, 2006," http://whitehouse.georgewbush.org/ask/jfalwell.asp.

CALIFORNIA'S NEXT CENTURY 2.0

Hollywood is a source of all that is wrong in America. "Falwell on the 'moral pervert[s]' in Hollywood: '[Y]ou almost got to be a homosexual to be recognized in the entertainment industry anymore.'"[83] Pat Robertson, Falwell's colleague and also a national religious leader, said that California in general is essentially evil.[84]

In 2007, national media host Glen Beck said, "[A] handful of people who hate America…are losing their homes in a forest fire today," referring to fires

---

[83] Media Matters, 2006; Also see: Christine Moers, "Jerry Falwell Still Believes Christians Are Being Duped by Global Warming"; "Falwell Says It is Anti-American to Oppose War" Public Theology, 2003; "Falwell Wages War on Two Fronts Against Celebrities, Committed Gay Couples," Right Wing Watch, 2006.

[84] Peter Jamison, "Does California ALSO Have a Pact With the Devil? We Ask Pat Robertson's Spokesman," SF Weekly, January 15, 2010.

that killed and maimed people and destroyed homes in Southern California.[85]

---

[85] "Beck: "[A] Handful of People Who Hate America…Are Losing Their Homes in a Forest Fire Today," Media Matters, October 27, 2007.

CALIFORNIA'S NEXT CENTURY 2.0

In 2009, Examiner.com, a major online newspaper, ran an article with the title, "I Really Don't Care Much About California, But This Stunned Me (The Sequel)" by William Dupray.

In 2010, Free Republic, a major online newspaper, asked if people hate California in "Hate California? Think CA is done? A lost cause? Watch this video of Cody and his flag." Also, that same year, in an attempt to gain national fundraising for a campaign in California, senatorial candidate Carly Fiorina said that the then current senator hates America.

The strongest evidence is the most anecdotal in nature, but largest in size: an Internet search of the phrase "why do people hate California" will literally turn up pages and pages of Internet postings, while the same phrase with any other state won't turn up more than one page, or any pages at all.

Perhaps the most telling proof is that when California asked for bailout, the national press erupted in controversy. Multiple news agencies said that California did not deserve a bailout because it overspent due to its own greed and lack of discipline, a result of the long-term, undisciplined, super liberal character of the state.[86] Hotair.com reported, "California hoped that their dire economic predicament might get

---

[86] "Rasmussen: 55% Say Better for California to Go Bankrupt Than Be Bailed Out," *Rasmussen Reports*, January 4, 2010; Rich Karlgaard, "Will Obama Bail Out California?" *Forbes.com*, May 21, 2009; Ron Elving, "Why Obama Has to Bail Out California, But Won't," *NPR*, June 23, 2009; Peter Nicholas and Richard Simon, "Washington Declines to Help California, at Least for Now," *Los Angeles Times*, May 22, 2009.

enough sympathy from the Obama administration to get a GM-style bailout. Sympathy, the White House has in abundance, but not cash—at least not for self-indulgent states who don't want to exercise some fiscal discipline. The White House finally drew the line on throwing cash at the insolvent."[87]

Forbes.com said, "Burdened by taxes and ever-growing regulation, the state is routinely rated by executives as having among the worst business climates in the nation. The problem could be demographic."[88]

---

[87] Ed Morrissey, "California Gets No Bailout Love from White House," HotAir.com, June 16, 2009, http://hotair.com/archives/2009/06/16/california-gets-no-bailout-love-from-white-house/.

[88] Joel Kotkin, "Who Killed California's Economy?" *Forbes.com*, July 6, 2009.

CALIFORNIA'S NEXT CENTURY 2.0

What is a mystery is how all of these news reporters and national news agencies forgot that California was price gouged by the Enron corporation under the protection of the federal government in 2001, a story that was carried across America by national news stations. And they forgot that California entered into this global recession with a deficit caused by this, a situation no other state had to deal with. Furthermore, they neglected to remind readers that the money that California was asking for was only a fraction of the extra federal tax money that it pays every year to states who are in better shape than California (another news item that has been covered across the nation by multiple national news agencies). How did all of these national news agencies forget this news that had been so widely reported only years before? The dynamic

of othering would provide an direct explanation:

news agencies and news reporters didn't report

these facts, although widely known in their

profession, because it went against their and the

nation's preconceived image of California, a land

of no spending discipline and full of illegal

aliens.

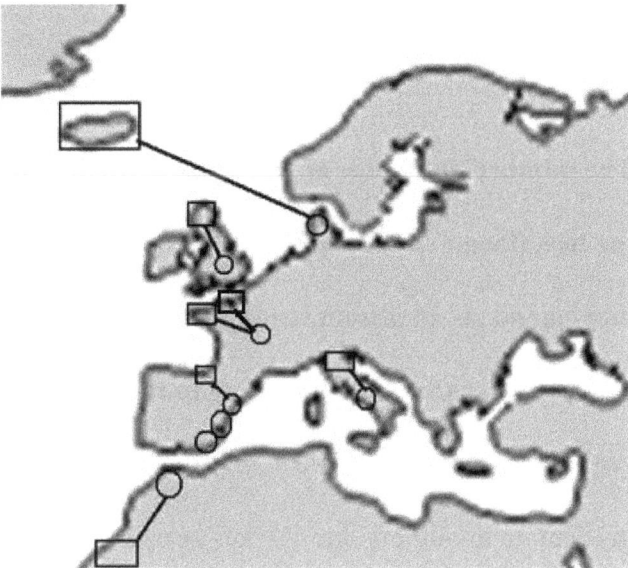

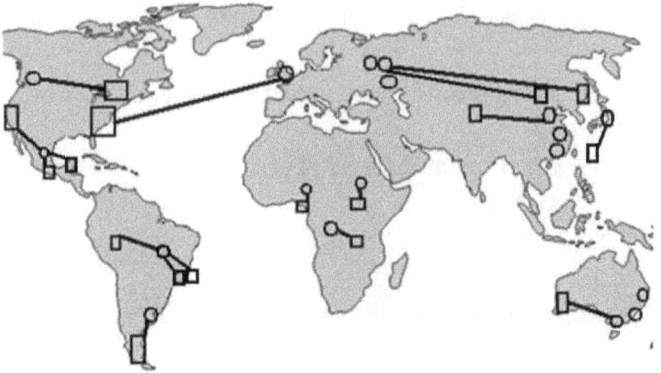

Independence movements from central powers, around the world

Circle = capital of nation, center of power

Square = distant area of nation trying to pull away

from center of power

The number one cause of secession, according to the best documented study of all modern movements, is an absent landlord who did not give extra resources or financing to the outlying region to keep it part. The administrative center gives more to outliers than it takes because the outliers are far from the center and therefore have more difficulty in participating in decision making and receiving support from the central government.[89] "...And those who are farther away would pay a lower tax."[90] In Canada, Italy, and Sweden, those areas that are farther away receive more money from the core than they give.[91] "However, individuals far away from the administrative center of the country (i.e., removed from the administrative center of government in preferences and location) could vote to break up the country because they do not experience the benefits

[89] Allen Buchanan, *Secession: The Morality of Political Divorce From Fort Sumter to Lithuania and Quebec* (Westview press, 1991).

[90] Ibid., 38.

[91] Enrico Spolaore and Albert Alesina, *The Size of Nations* (MIT Press, 2005), 52.

of public goods as much as closer regions in preferences to government policy making."[92]

America's history with California for last thirty years has been the exact opposite of successful behavior for keeping distant provinces as part of the union. This is not a unique situation; many other countries' capitals did not pay sufficient attention or support to distant regions and, as a result, dealt with secession movements.

Examples of the secession movements include (from the maps above):

[92] Donatella Della Porta and Mario Dani Blackwell, *Social Movements: An Introduction* (Wiley-Blackwell, 2006), 12, 197. Also the concept is discussed in (Leopold Kohr, *The Breakdown of Nations* (Green Books Ltd., 1957), 64–65).

CALIFORNIA'S NEXT CENTURY 2.0

South Sudan in Sudan; South Congo in Congo;
Sahel in Morocco; Normandy and Brittany in
France; North Italy in Italy; America and England;
California, Chiapas, and Yucatan from the center of
Mexico; Basque in Spain; Iceland and Denmark;
Scotland and England, Biafra in Nigeria; Western
Australia in Australia; Quebec in Canada;
Vladivostok in Russia; Xinjiang in China;
Priamurye in Russia; Ryukya in Japan;
Riograndense and the Juliana Republic and Acre
state in Brazil; and Kingdom of Araucania and
Patagonia in Argentina.

(It should be noted that this gap can never be
closed. There was a centuries-long effort to
populate the western half of America, with the
federal Homestead Act of 1862. Ranches that were

bought west of the current border of the MAP, the I-35 freeway, are mostly abandoned, leaving only trees marking out the borders of ranches long abandoned. The census records show a loss of population across the gigantic western half of the country from the late 1800s and continuing to today. Americans don't want to live in the West, and those who did have almost all left. A federal government report on this trend estimated that the cost to repopulate the West to where it was just a few decades ago would be similar to the entire cost of the Iraq war to date.)

APPENDIX II:

How renaissance is actually possible

Two different areas in the world, two different times, two different systems equals the same dynamic catalyzing in renaissance, aka, forcing multiple sources of diverse knowledge and culture into a confined spac

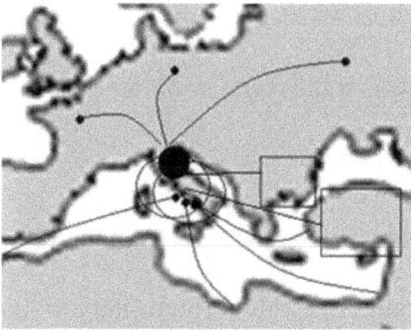

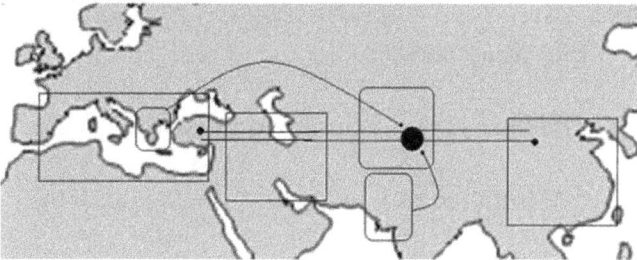

CALIFORNIA'S NEXT CENTURY 2.0

The classical Renaissance started in the city-state of Florence, Italy, in the late 1400s. It started because of the convergence of these nineteen conditions:

1. Byzantine Empire crumbled—lost knowledge was literally flowing out.

2. Turks were on the run from lost territory.

3. Greeks were on the run from lost territory.

4. Italy had abandoned Arab Moorish libraries.

5. Italy had Roman libraries that were forgotten.

6. Northern Italy was trade route to northern Europe.

7. All trade in Mediterranean and Baltic Sea cultural areas came through northern Italy to the European market.

8. Florence's main industry was textiles—using dye from the east and wool from the north to

make unique finished products that depended on world trade materials.

9. Wealthy developed a culture where it was as important to invest in art as economic commercial activity.

10. Florence was a stable republic.

11. Florence was highly urbanized at this time.

12. Social mobility was high.

13. Based on work, artists could become middle class or wealthy.

14. Social inequality was high—there were many patrons.

15. Large middle class developed with a strong taste for foreign goods.

16. Laws banning trade with all non-Christians were repealed.

17. Inability of church to provide relief to Black Death plague rocked the masses' belief in the church, and many people became open to secular ideas.

18. Labor costs went up because population had shrunk, so people made good money on labor.

19. However, production of fine products went up when resources' cost went down because less people demanded resources.

Generalized, these nineteen conditions can be boiled down to thirteen conditions:

1. Old empire was falling down. Its knowledge brokers, the main scholars, were leaving on their own and looking for new homes. All of these high-value scholars in the old society found themselves without jobs that pay.

2. At least two different cultural scholars were looking for new jobs.

3. The city had two different types of educational libraries that were ignored.

4. City was the trade link between two different giant trade blocs, the Mediterranean and northern Europe.

5. City had already developed strong industry that was dependent on foreign trade for goods—import dependent.

6. This industry base produced fine finished products that were sold internationally—main export.

7. City had strong domestic consumer base that liked international goods.

8. Elites had culture of supporting arts and culture for the entire city.

9. Large middle class had money to spend.

10. Skilled labor was paid well.

11. Cheap raw resources were available.

12. Trade barriers against most of world were removed.

13. Mass of people were looking for something new to put their faith, dreams, hopes, and passions into.

These thirteen can be further boiled down to just seven conditions:

1. Big middle class with money to spend and likes foreign goods.

2. Elites who pride themselves on sponsoring culture.

3. City is already a world trade nexus—bringing goods in, shipping them to other locations,

making combined finish products for export-

dependent economy.

4. Two types of whole education systems being
   explored locally.

5. Two types of giant knowledge spheres unable to
   pay high wages to their professors.

6. A crumbling empire right next door with all
   knowledge flowing out at cheap prices.

7. Stable government and positive society, people
   believing in society because government is
   rational and stable.

Of 1,500 documented cultures around the world in

the last ten thousand years of human existence,[1]

there have been only seven to nine cultures at

different places, in different times, that could be

---

[1] *Encyclopedia of World Culture* (1996).

said to meet the conditions for a renaissance:
Florence, Italy, during the end of the medieval
period of Europe; Alhambra in southern Spain
during late reign of Moorish Muslims over
Christian Spain; Cahokia on the center of the
Mississippi River in America, pre-European
contact; Late Byzantine Empire after Rome fell and
during the Ottoman Muslim conquest of Europe;
Athens in Greece during the Greek golden age;
Kushan Empire in Bagram in central Afghanistan
during the later half of the Silk Road era; Baghdad
in Iraq during the medieval period of Europe shortly
after the birth of Islam and toward the end of the
Roman Empire. There is some evidence that Tibet,
after the fall of the first Tibetan Empire and before
the invasion of the Mongols, also achieved a
renaissance. There is also evidence for an extremely

limited renaissance of high priests in southern France, 900–1000 AD, referred to as the Carolingian Renaissance.

Cultures that have achieved renaissance are .5–.6% of all human cultures since the first records of human culture. While exceptionally rare, their existence proves that this condition can be recreated across all cultures in the world when the conditions are right.

Alhambra was the trading port between the Muslim world at its peak and all of Europe. It was home to Christians, Muslims, Jews, and atheists, all who worked together freely in a close-knit international port economy. Muslim rulers at this time valued beautiful architecture mosques to spread their faith, and they believed that the sign of elite status was based on the size of a person's library. Because the Alhambra region at this time was small, only skilled labor could be afforded and most raw materials had to be imported in. Alhambra was the education destination for any person in all of North Africa and all of Europe who wanted to get an education in any subject. It attracted teachers wanting a good salary and students with ambition throughout the western Mediterranean region.

Cahokia is a culture that is only recently being given the attention that it deserves. The city was a trade point at the connection of the Mississippi, Missouri, and Illinois rivers, connecting the cultures of literally the entire eastern half of America, from the midwestern states to the East Coast to the South.

CALIFORNIA'S NEXT CENTURY 2.0

It was arranged in four to five giant cultural groups, each with their own crop and natural resource products. Although there are no written records, evidence suggests a capital the size of London or Paris during the same time period of 1200 AD. The Cahokia employed engineering, had astrological understanding, traded massively in finished goods, traded with money minted in the capital, and used a complex burial system that suggested a highly complex and ordered society.

The late Byzantine Empire, on the edge of Turkey, was also a small area. When Rome fell, all of the scholars and skilled laborers of Rome went to Byzantium, the only place they could find work for their skills. The area was also a port city that connected the Baltic Sea with Slavic cultures to the

ancient Mediterranean Sea with Levant cultures.
Although constantly fighting the Muslim Ottoman
Empire, it traded with the empire and grabbed
knowledge from this enemy empire when it could.
It also traded with Vikings from the far north. The
empire was constantly inspired by the largest and
most beautiful building in the ancient world at the
time, the Hagia Sophia located in the center of the
capital.

Athens was the main city of the Greek city-states
during the height of Greece. It was a port city
dedicated to trade positioned between the Baltic Sea
and Slavic cultures to the north and the ancient
Mediterranean Sea and cultures. Greek scholars
traveled throughout Egypt, whose empire had
fallen, and took many books from forgotten libraries

and built on the knowledge. Also, although threatened by the powerful Persian Empire that ruled 2/3rds of the known world, it also inspired the Greeks to look to new solutions and technologies. This was also the time of the greatest extent of Greek exploration, reaching far into Russia, Egypt, Libya, Israel, and Italy. Greek sailors brought back strange stories and goods; their stories were retold in heroic fashion, inspiring generations of young Greeks. Scholars arose to record these stories mostly for entertainment, and a thriving market for plays and stories arose. Also, while threatened, the Greek islands had maintained a strong sense of local democracy and security from foreign invasion.

The Kushan Empire, long ignored by scholars, has only recently gained attention, being recognized as a fascinating hybrid culture. It was formed in the near center of the Silk Road, a distance away from any strong empire, giving it great unquestioned authority in its region. Goods brought from the Roman Empire, Persian Empire, and Chinese Empire all met at the Kushan capital. Here they were switched to be traded to the other side of the Silk Road or combined into refined products and sold to the empires. The empire merged together art and philosophy and science from all three empires, as well as adopting local culture of the region, which had heavily been influenced by earlier Greek immigrants. Later the empire moved into northern India and grabbed Indian culture into its mix. Because of its location at the center of a worldwide trade line, it began minting and distributing its own currency to trading partners.

Baghdad became the intellectual capital of the entire Muslim Empire, 900–1300 AD. Greek, Indian, Persian, and Arab culture all merged together in one city of nearly one million people. Because of this, all scholars from southern Europe to western India traveled to one city to learn or be taught. The Persian Empire had recently been conquered resulting in the merging of overwhelmingly Persian with Arab cultures in Baghdad. The greatest Persian scholars lived and taught advanced sciences while Rome was in decline thereby providing many scholars from these dying empires the only place they could find the best paying jobs. New methods of sea navigation created much easier travel to distant lands, and at the same time, the development of paper spread into the Middle East from China, leading to knowledge being spread in vast distances and reports from around the world converging in one educational metropolis. Invasions by Mongols and Christian crusaders, but specifically the destruction of libraries and schools along with a period of ineffective government, created the destruction of this Renaissance.

Timbuktu was the capital trading city of two empires who overlapped each other, the Mali and the Songhay. It was the central distribution point for the Tuareg trading caravans that traversed the entire North African continent trading goods. Between three different trading regimes, it became a center place for literature and record keeping, housing one

the best libraries in history until it was raided by
another tribe who had envied its knowledge.
Toward the end of its height, Alhambra Muslims
from southern Spain, a mixed culture on its own,
also traveled to Timbuktu and worked as knowledge
workers.

These stories are important because they illustrate
clearly the similarities that created these
renaissances among regions and cultures that were
very different from each other. These similarities
include:

1. An international trade nexus that brings
   goods in from at least two to three different
   giant trading regions and redistributes them,
   also making a local economy dependent on

international trade logistics and refined products for sale to the giant trading blocs.

2. A highly skilled labor economy with good wages, creating a middle class that is based on creating art and trade products.

3. One to two collapsed empires nearby where the scholars can't find work in their old homes.

4. Access to whole educational libraries that are not currently valued

5. Two to five different cultures being used as stock for social conventions, education, philosophy, and religion. Includes a welcoming environment for all of these immigrants, enabling them to find good jobs and paying well to teach.

6. Sponsoring literature, arts, or research are seen as signs of elite status.

7. A stable government. Either the government can be under military threat by an outside power but able to hold its borders securely even if it is smaller than the outside threat, or the government can have no significant border threats.

This analysis is key because it brings to light the fact that California has the ability to recreate all of the conditions to become the world's eighth or eleventh renaissance in all of human history or in the last five hundred years. Consider the following:

- California is already a trading nexus between three giant and very different trade blocs—Latin America, America, and Asia.

CALIFORNIA'S NEXT CENTURY 2.0

- California already has an economy dependent on international trade for materials; it also develops refined goods from combined materials from around the world (the airline industry in California and computer industry are good examples).

- California is already full of immigrants from many different regional societies—Latino, Asian, American, Indian.

- California already has a large middle class that has a strong taste for foreign goods.

- California already has a strong artistic domestic culture.

- California already has a Californianized elite class.

- California has a stable government— although it could be more peaceful and less divisive, the state has never been invaded, and people do not feel in fear of any invasion.

- California has schools, universities, and professors developed by the Chinese and Latin communities, which are currently overlooked and not valued by mainstream culture.

- With the shrinking Russian and American empires, many experts from these empires are unable to find jobs employing their high skills like they could in the recent past.

Most of the conditions already exist, and the conditions that do not exist already have strong bases to launch from. California would need to do a couple things to start a renaissance:

CALIFORNIA'S NEXT CENTURY 2.0

1. Hire experts from the old empires of America and Russia to come and teach subjects those empires excelled at, paying them more than they can get in the old empires.

2. California's elites have to sponsor arts and knowledge and make it the standard of elitism. .

3. California has to value, as a society, Latino and Chinese knowledge bases.

In addition it could improve things that it already doing:

1. Create less volatility in government and politics.

2. Encourage greater immigration from the large trading blocs of India, Russia, and

Brazil, as Europe, America, and China are already represented strongly.

3. Increase its role as a global trade nexus.

The key point to take away is that all of these conditions are exceptionally achievable. They are not theoretical concepts but things all of the mass population can understand and what the mass of California already see happening. Fundamentally, there is no radically new concept to introduce to society at all.

Furthermore, two results from this attempt to bring about renaissance make it likely that California would pursue transforming to the world's eighth renaissance: A) it gives elites the role of being leaders and inspirers of the masses, a role of importance where society counts on them and looks up to them, and B) it gives the masses a fantastic goal—to live and be creative to make a creative society by being part of the mass society.

All of this leads to a powerful nexus of conclusion: the plan to make California into the new Switzerland for the next century as the main industry of California will create all of the conditions needed to catapult California into a renaissance.

Near complete control over local decisions, the exuberance and exaltation that will come from this development—the feeling of empowerment that California is going to and can take control of herself—added to being the world foci point for discussion and debates on all of the important issues of the next age would create the conditions for a new renaissance to be born specifically within the bounds of California.

Every renaissance requires elites to participate to even happen. California can be no exception. In California it is too popular to criticize the rich just for being rich. We don't separate those who earned their wealth all on their own, or through innovation, from the ones who simply inherited it and squander their wealth. Rather, revealing the emotionality of this dynamic, all rich are criticized in California.

In the past, there have been examples where the elite provided leadership, inspiration, and a vision because they knew they had so much and they wanted to at least make life a step better for all of their countrymen. Franklin Delano Roosevelt, Eleanor Roosevelt, Teddy Roosevelt, and Clysthenies, who founded Greek democracy, are all examples.

California, on its own, historically also has had these elites, such as, Mariano Vallejo and Joaquin Murrieta. And even today, California still has a history of the wealthy working in the public realm to make life better when they could have sat back and just enjoyed their wealth: Ron Unz, Darrel Issa, and Arnold Schwarzenegger.

There is an old term in the English language for a wealthy elite who chooses to help the public, who sees it as their public duty to provide leadership and inspiration, to use their mind and, at times, their own finances to make the difference needed to push through. In the past, the word used was *patrician*. Today, indicative of the loss of this historical role, the word for the wealthy is simply *elite* or *the one percent*. The people listed above are just some recent examples of this trend that exists in California still.

Wouldn't it be great if rich people in California cared about the mass of California in general? If they returned to the historic duty of the wealthy in all great Western societies (from London to Athens)? It could happen. It has happened for centuries in the past across the world's cultures. And in order for renaissance to occur in California, this condition literally must return.

During the Renaissance of Italy in the 1500s, the elites, the kings and queens, barons, and rich merchants all sponsored the arts, and all talked about how great the arts were. The public listened directly to these people, looked up to them for leadership, and talked about how to make art themselves at every chance they had in a conversation. A million conversations over coffee at a café during the Renaissance created art, science, and literature as we know it now. The kings could hire the best artists and could deliver the best speeches, but it was the mass feeding off this group vision (sponsored financially and ideologically by the kings and wealthy) that created the mass of ideas that created the Renaissance.

California will have to enact this dynamic society again. The good news is that it already has prominent examples, mentioned above, and, according to the most recent surveys of the wealthy, a population ripe for taking on this grand duty.

According to the *New York Times* in "The Richest of the Rich, Proud of a New Gilded Age," the majority of the new super wealthy are not motivated by dollars but by the challenge of building a business and are still greatly motivated by being a leader to society to help it develop like philanthropists of old. "The money is a byproduct of a passionate endeavor." Adding to this point, that the super wealthy already are a people motivated by philanthropy in general, another article ("I'm for the Rich," published in the *National Review*), says the top 10% of the population pays for 25% of all donations. And another article ("To the New Rich, Bill's OK," published by AEI Online), says that California is already holding a vast natural reserve of this particular type of resource, that of the new super wealthy, stating boldly that the majority of the new super rich live in California alone.

How to reconnect the masses to the wealthy and the wealthy to their historic roles in great Western societies is not a clear-cut path. But it is something that must happen if the full dream of California's next century is to bloom, and it is one that California already has all the requisite parts to enact.

APPENDIX III:

Addressing concerns with an independent California

1. This is not a secession war—it is a proposal for a rearrangement of partnership. The war for secession in America was about states who voluntarily joined America wanting to leave through the use of military force. The Confederate states did two things right away to directly create the Civil War that are virtually impossible with the proposals of this book, specifically of subnational sovereignty. First, they printed their own money and began issuing it among themselves, and they formed an army, declared it an independent army, and then lead

an attack against a US military base at Fort Sumter. Under the proposal described here, both of these actions are impossible. This is all beside the point that the Confederacy was about preserving a specific economic system that was at odds with the economy of the rest of America (slave labor versus skilled manufacturing), whereas this proposal is to develop a new economy that will substantially grow the American economy through its link. Furthermore, California is not part of one large population body that had been connected for centuries before attempting to split. Southern colonies interacted with northern colonies for centuries before the federal government of America was ever formed. Trade and trade routes were already established. Trade and interaction only increased after the combined colonies of America formed a formal federal government, which lasted for almost two centuries before having its union challenged. California has always been a population apart with little interaction with the rest of the America; for centuries before it was part of the Union, and for a full century after, it was part of the Union, until nearly the 1950s. There was never a period of routine interaction because of the vast geographic population gap between the population of California and MAP.

2. This will not hurt the economy—because trade and security aren't touched at all. Existing trade and business agreements will stay the same. Changes to trade agreements will be worked out

in slow (i.e., small pieces at a time between individual companies as they choose) methodical rate that changes to business contracts have traditionally taken. Although, there will now be a border check at California— even this is not new: California already has border checkpoints with all states and already stops all traffic coming into the state to examine cars for fresh fruits and produce. Mechanically the process for entering and leaving an independent California is already in place. Furthermore, California's economy will grow once independent because trade will grow, due to the new focus on foreign trade, philosophically, politically, and financially; also it will be able to design its laws and economy to fit international trade at the speed that it wants

CALIFORNIA'S NEXT CENTURY 2.0

instead of waiting for years as it currently has

to. This will increase the quality of products and

services that California can provide to the

international market. Which will increase

foreign trade with California. Because

California is economically linked to America,

trade with America will increase because now

California would have an increased economy.

Therefore Americas economy will grow

indirectly from California's independence,

because of their continue economic link. Also,

given the connections to the world's nations and

trade blocks that California would gain access to

as the New Switzerland for this next century,

there will be even more increased trade with

California, which again because it is linked to

America will indirectly increase Americas

economic activity.

Consequently, USA's economy will automatically grow with California independence, as trade will grow automatically because of the internal and historical link to California trade. **Trade between Scotland and England and, especially, between Hong Kong and China have not gone down in the last decades. Since devolving, their countries have actually shown increased economic growth on their own and with trade with the original home country.**[1] Also note that Scotland had it

---

[1] Gillian Bowditch, "Undervaluing Independence Makes Monkeys out of Us All," *Sunday Times of London*, November 12, 2011; Bill Jamieson, "Threat to Top Credit Rating in Separate Scotland," *The Scotsman*, April 1, 2012; *Economic and Trade Information on Hong Kong, 27 3 2012*, (The Hong Kong Trade Development Council 2012)

troops' valor praised by the queen of England

for their fighting service in the recent

Afghanistan war, which they participated in

after subnational sovereignty was achieved for

Scotland.[2]

3. This is not radical—Scotland and Hong Kong

    are very financially conservative countries with

    very strong economies, and both have done this.

    Note that, as proof of their commitment to

    strong economics, Scottish people invented the

    concept of economics first (Adam Smith),

    developed the banking system in other nations

    of major power (France's banking industry was

---

[2] "Queen Honours 3 SCOTS Soldiers," Defense News, July 15, 2010,
http://www.mod.uk/DefenceInternet/DefenceNews/HistoryAndHonour/QueenHonours3ScotsSoldiers.htm

created by John Law, a Scotsman), and Hong Kong is routinely held up as the perfect example of what all economies should be (by the American economist Milton Freedman).

4. This is not something that can expand. It is limited only to nations that had governments before joining the Union, were taken by military force against their will, and are able to be effective governments (and not immediately moved into a situation of economic despair similar to Swaziland in South Africa or Haiti in the Caribbean). Very few places meet the first half of the conditions, and exceptionally few places meet the second half after they have meet the first half—this leaves literally the Navajo, the Lakota, California, and Hawaii. Allowing all

natives to have independent lands when they are not of a high enough density within a small geography will create nations where the people are essentially all extremely rural. Nations like these do not work; Mali, Niger, Botswana, Chad, Mongolia, and Kazakhstan are all examples of countries that seem to be permanently poor and backwards compared to their regional neighbors. The fact that North Carolina natives were included proves that America wanted to make the most amount of people free that it "workably could." While other territories that make up America have been taken by military force, there was not an official government there, there was no substantial population in the area to make an effective government (Colorado, Nevada, New

Mexico, and Arizona), or the nations were sold by their superior government (Louisiana), or they attacked America (Florida), or they joined the Union of their own free will (Texas).

5. The plan for sub-national sovereignty for California but not full classical independence is the perfect balance— as exemplified by situation in Scotland: although there were some Scottish people who wanted full independence from Britain, this was overwhelmingly voted as too radical for most Scots. The debate on full independence and no independence is what caused Scotland to look into a new option. Subnational sovereignty was created and popularized by Alex Salmon, a head politician who won control of the national Scottish

political party pushing for a change, after he rearranged the political discussion in Scotland to be more about financial equality than needing increased independence for purely social/cultural reasons. Basing the discussion on solid reasons instead of emotional ones and designing the independence to keep key ties to the mother country are what allowed Scotland to move past a long debate (for the last thirty years, since 1970) into actual policy (within the last five, since 2005).

6. If California is allowed to devolve, then what is to stop California counties from wanting to devolve further? The answer is twofold: A) it is already widely recognized in California that counties have too much independent power, and

this has seriously helped cause the routine political confusion in Sacramento, and B) there have been 220 campaigns to split California into different regions since the Gold Rush, and at least a couple campaigns to do the same when the Spanish were in charge of California— making this a political issue that goes back 300 years—and it has never happened. Furthermore, according to sociologists who have studied the state, there are seven to twelve recognized regions of California (only two of which are the Bay Area and Los Angeles), and all of these regions view themselves as uniquely different from all of the other regions. Only the Bay Area and Los Angeles view the state as being split just between their two cultural regions of California.

CALIFORNIA'S NEXT CENTURY 2.0

IMAGE

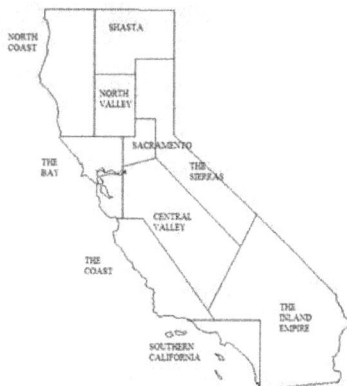

REALITY

CALIFORNIA'S NEXT CENTURY 2.0

Details on the competitive advantage of being the new Switzerland for the new century

CALIFORNIA CAN ESTABLISH A COMPETITIVE ADVANTAGE OR PERMANENT DOMINANCE WITH THIS PLAN BASED ON THE BEST THEORISTS OF ECONOMICS

The plan to be the new Switzerland for the Next Century relies on a country being comfortable with diversity. As shown before, California has the greatest strength in this area, of any nation in the world. California people have lived diversely so long that it is who Californians are. This inherent character can be the main tool, skill, and resource that California builds its main industry on.

Only those able to match the level of inherent diversity of basic identity can compete for becoming the new Switzerland as California can. And as shown in Chapter 4 only a few small nations in the world have a level of history of diversity, even in a rough comparative range, with California.

Added to the fact that the world is showing signs of becoming more xenophobic and having flatlined with immigration and travel, it is reasonable to expect that no new nations will become diverse inherently any time soon, and in fact the entire world may become less diverse and progressive in the near future. Even if nations started programs now to become diverse, it will take thirty years for that society to adapt and adopt diversity into its basic identity. There is a recognized twenty-five-plus year gap for any societies conducting massive change.[1]

Regardless, diversity in a society and accepting of diversity inherently in any society will continue to be rare. This is because people naturally don't like to interact with other cultures and tend to shy away from it, and many diverse societies that have been historically diverse can't seem to make it work. "This finding is consistent with recent research demonstrating that intergroup contact is mentally challenging and cognitively draining, and consistent

---

[1] *Global Trends 2025: A Transformed World* (National Intelligence Council, 2008)

with findings that contact reduces prejudice,"[2]

Those diverse societies that like it and excel in their diversity and, most importantly, see it as inherently part of their identity are in a league of their own across the entire world. A tiny league unlikely to expand greatly. In this tiny league, California excels beyond all other areas.

With an industry based on inherent, tested, diversity, all of the world is flat compared to California.

---

[2] Stephanie Pappas, "Low IQ & Conservative Beliefs Linked to Prejudice," *LiveScience.com,* January 26 2012, http://news.yahoo.com/low-iq-conservative-beliefs-linked-prejudice-180403506.html

CALIFORNIA'S NEXT CENTURY 2.0

HOW CALIFORNIA MEETS MICHAEL PORTER'S CONCEPT OF "THE COMPETITIVE ADVANTAGE OF NATIONS"

By developing a community of competing businesses in a localized area of the nation—all focused on a niche industry, unique in the world—a whole nation can dominate an entire global industry. Free competition exists between these industries, but they create a community that, with encouragement by that nation (sometimes direct and sometimes just in spirit), can secure unquestioned dominance in an industry seemingly for decades or even centuries. Author Michael Porter, in his book *The Competitive Advantage of Nations*, shows how across different nations, this same dynamic has secured industries from 30–150 years for different countries by creating industry communities that simply no other one firm or nation can compete with, seemingly forever. (Competitive advantage of some of the national examples of industries only ended when the world changed, as the creation of the assembly line in the 1800s stopped the need for handcrafted watches that had existed since medieval times.) A country takes something that is already somewhat good at and then localizes the industry or components of the industry with the entire nation, bringing those subcomponents together to make the final product. While highly academic in concept, Californians should already be familiar with the concept as it is an exact description of the Silicon Valley computer industry in San Jose, California.[3]

---

[3] "Diamond Model—Competitive Advantage of Nations," www.provenmodel.com, accessed May 3, 2012,

CALIFORNIA'S NEXT CENTURY 2.0

Porter defined four main conditions as the keys to figuring out what a nation's competitive advantage could be: factor conditions (its natural skill sets and resources), demand conditions (products that the home market already has high demand for), supporting industries (presence of existing industries related to the goal), and existing firm organizational structure and strategy. Furthermore, he listed two more conditions that could help: chance events (global events that provide opportunity for the nation), and government (how much help the government gives and the government's understanding of not interfering in a successful industry).

---

http://www.provenmodels.com/577/diamond-model---
competitive-advantage-of-nations/porter,-michael-e

CALIFORNIA'S NEXT CENTURY 2.0

California meets all of these determinate conditions. California is already diverse. It has a large population of people from the new superpower countries of the world who routinely demand travel, communication, goods, and art and science products from those countries. California has firms that already specialize in working with overseas companies on international products; these firms also have a history of fierce competition for international customers among themselves. In addition, the world is rapidly changing and is already showing signs of needing a global negotiation hub (and the government of California has already issued reports analyzing how to promote international trade and the international presence of the state for the last twenty-five years). This is, at minimum, a thoroughly strong platform to launch the California industry into being the new Switzerland for the next century as based on what is near universally considered the new manual on global economics (The Competitive Advantage of Nations).

QUOTES FROM THE COMPETITIVE ADVANTAGE OF NATIONS:

- "Creating advantage...it can be manifested in product changes, process changes, new approaches to marketing, new forms of distribution, and new conceptions of scope...it depends more on a culmination of small insights and advances than on major technological breakthroughs." (pg. 45)

- "Competitive advantage is often created or shifts when buyers develop new needs or their priorities change significantly. Established competitors may fail to perceive the new needs or be unable to respond because meeting the demands a new value chain." (pg. 46)

- "Early movers gain advantages such as being first to reap economies of scale, reducing costs through cumulative learning, establishing brand names, and customer relationships without direct competition, getting their pick of distribution channels, and obtaining the best locations..." (pg. 47)

- "Often innovators are 'outsiders' in some way, to the existing industry." (pg. 48)

- "...change is extraordinarily painful and difficult for any successful organization. Complacency is more natural. The past strategy becomes ingrained in organizational routines. Information that would modify or challenge it is not sought or filtered out. The past strategy takes on an aura of invincibility and becomes rooted in company culture. Suggestion change is tantamount to disloyalty. (pg. 48)"

- "Another important motivation for dispersing activities is to enhance local marketing in a foreign nation, by signaling commitment to local buyers and or providing greater local responsiveness." (pg. 56)

- "Swiss ability to deal with different languages and cultures…is an advantage in services such as banking, trading, and logistics management." (pg. 76)

CALIFORNIA'S NEXT CENTURY 2.0

- "The most significant and sustainable competitive advantage results when a nation possesses factors needed for competing in a particular industry that are both advanced and specialized." (pg. 79)

- "A nation's firms then become early and aggressive movers in dealing with problems that will be widespread. A good example is Switzerland." (pg. 83)

- "Nations gain competitive advantage in industries or industry segments where their demand gives local firms a clearer or earlier picture of buyer needs than foreign rivals can have."[4] (pg 86)

---

[4] California has world culture getting along here.

- "Travel has a long tradition and is a way of life in countries such Sweden and Switzerland...for example founders of an important company had been trained or had lived for a long time outside Switzerland before returning home. Inevitably, one of the founders' first acts was to establish a foreign subsidiary in the country where he or she had lived. Both Swedish and Swiss firms do well in competing in industries requiring far flung global strategies and involving sensitive relations with local governments and buyers." (pg. 109)

- "When an industry takes on the status of national priority and or prestigious place to work, talented people flow into it and demonstrate unusual commitment and effort." (pg. 114)

- "...nations tend to be competitive in activities that are admired or depended upon; that is, where the heroes come from." (pg. 115)

- "Preserving advantage may well require reinvesting all available profits in a major restructuring despite low current returns and in the face of substantial risk. Innovations are frequently more necessary at times when current profitability is down." (pg. 116)

- "Social norms and values affect the nature of home demand, for example, as well as the goals of managers and the way firms are organized. Social and political history influence the skills that have been accumulated in a nation and the institutional structure within with competition operations. These aspects of a nation, which some call culture, cannot be separated from economic outcomes." (pg. 129)

- UC-Davis is presented as example of concept working in California (pg. 134)

- Hollywood is presented as example of concept working in California (pg.139)

- In service industries, the top three are UK, US, and Switzerland as equals. (pg. 254)

- This equality of tiny Switzerland with larger countries in international business is because of their inherent language and cultural skills (pg. 257)

- "Swiss firms do well where trust, discretion and personalized attention are important, or complex negotiations among parties are essential." (pg. 264)

- Switzerland sits on top of the world market regardless of its size because of its culture of innovation and global outreach. (pgs. 712–714)

It should be noted that it was directly admitted by the California state government that diversity was the state's competitive advantage in the report. *California Trade And Investment Strategy—Roles for the State in Global Market Development by The California Business, Transportation and Housing Agency*: "Section 2.2.1—Competitive advantage and its bearing on state economic development strategy...California is unusual in that the diversity of its competitive attributes is so great that this itself is a competitive advantage."

HOW THIS PLAN FOR CALIFORNIA MEETS THE OTHER TENETS OF THE OTHER MAJOR ECONOMIC THEORIES SINCE THE BEGINNING OF ECONOMICS

Adam Smith—1776—Absolute Advantage

(Through specializing on development of a product and service—by being able to do that thing better and more than anyone else—a country secures its industry.)

- Some countries can produce good more efficiently than others.

- Global production is maximized therefore through global free trade.

CALIFORNIA'S NEXT CENTURY 2.0

- Real wealth is based directly on goods and services available to citizens, not the holding of gold reserves (Singapore vs. Indonesia).

- Countries can increase their efficiency through specialization.

- Economy of scale—number of times you do the process well equals how productive and cheap you can make the product.

- No time lost acquiring new skill, technology.

- Focusing on a few productions inevitably brings the eye for process improvement.

- Climate conditions allow for some agriculture products to be made most efficiently in certain places.

David Ricardo—1817—Comparative Advantage

(California does diversity and communication better

than anyone else—so it should focus on these as its main industry.)

- Built on Smith's thesis, countries should focus on products they can do more efficiently than others even if they can produce other products by themselves. It's better to buy from others those products they can produce less efficiently and instead focus on producing and making a profit on the things they can produce best.

Hecksher and Ohlin—1933—Factors Proportions Model (Focusing on diversity and making it work—especially because few others can do this at all—is the key California resource.)

- Factors that are scarce are more expensive than factors that are abundant; this determines a country's competitive advantage. Capital, labor, energy, raw resources, tourism—you should focus on what you have a lot of as the strategy for your economy.

(Large country acting small: Improving transportation in a large country to the point that it is the same speed as a small country gives the large country competitive advantage because it can provide more of the services a small country can, but there is no transportation speed loss. England and Japan did massive railway construction in home countries and throughout foreign world investments, way beyond other similar powers.)

Raymond Vernon—1966—Product Life Cycle

(This theory suggests Switzerland, the UN, and other organizations are naturally ending their useful lives.)

- Industries in an economy have a life cycle like everything else.

- Introduction—new product or skill introduced.

  (Adam Smith—advantage in quick to learn new product or technology)

- Growth—produce/skill still new, but being researched, expanded.

  (Adam Smith—advantage is in product specialization)

- Maturity—everyone who is anyone knows how to do this now.

  (Adam Smith, David Ricardo—drop industries that you cannot specialize in, be the only one or one of a few doing it)

- Decline—everything has been tried, everyone is in the market now.

CALIFORNIA'S NEXT CENTURY 2.0

Paul Krugman—1980—Country Size Theory

(Suggests that California could provide the role of the new Switzerland better than any of the five to seven pillars.)

- Large countries do less global trade than small countries because inherently they can produce most of the goods they need domestically. This is not an option for small countries.

- Distance between production and distribution sites requires farther transportation distances and therefore costs than small countries. Small countries can connect anywhere in their entire country for a comparatively small amount of money.

- Small countries have to invest globally because it is the only way they can build up a large enough market to spread the risks of having a business. Large countries have large domestic markets that are already stable, so they don't have to invest in foreign countries.

CALIFORNIA'S NEXT CENTURY 2.0

APPENDIX V:

Global Corporate tax rate and trade calculations

(This is only a rough calculation to show that moving the tax rate in California to a level that is recognized as globally competitive is possible. What the exact numbers would be is a topic that should be researched by the proposed California Blue Ribbon panel.)

Corporate tax

Corporate taxes in California in 2008 = 11.6% of California state budget, or $12B[5]

California corporate tax rate in 2008 = 8.84%[6]

---

[5] "General Fund Revenue: Corporate Tax" Governors Budget 2008-09 , accessed May 3, 2012, http://2008-09.archives.ebudget.ca.gov/BudgetSummary/REV/32270756.html.

Federal corporate taxes = 34–35%[7]

Federal spending after taxes received[8]

California state budget 2008 = $42B[9]

State budget is usually the amount of extra

federal tax rate of $42B[10]

---

[6] "2008 California Tax Rates and Exemptions" State of California Franchise Tax Board, accessed May 3, 2012,

https://www.ftb.ca.gov/forms/2008_california_tax_rates_an d_exemptions.shtml.

[7] "Corporate tax in the United States" Wikipedia.com, accessed May 3, 2012

http://en.wikipedia.org/wiki/Corporate_tax_in_the_United_S tates.

[8] "Federal Taxes Paid vs. Federal Spending Received by State, 1981-2005" Tax Foundation, accessed May 3, 2012,m http://www.taxfoundation.org/research/show/22685.html.

[9] "California Budget Historical Documents, 2008-09 " California Department of Finance, accessed May 3, 2012,

http://www.dof.ca.gov/budget/historical/2008-09/.

CALIFORNIA'S NEXT CENTURY 2.0

9% corporate tax in California in 2008 = $12B

$42B ÷ $12B = 3.5 x 9% = 31.5%

Total federal and California state corporate tax rate = 9% + 35% = 44%

44% - 31.5% (return on extra federal taxes) = 12.5% total corporate tax rate for California as own total.

Hong Kong tax rate = 16.5%

Singapore tax rate = 17%[11]

---

[10] **"Federal Taxes Paid vs. Federal Spending Received by State, 1981-2005" Tax Foundation, accessed May 3, 2012,** http://www.taxfoundation.org/research/show/22685.html.

[11] **"List of countries by tax rates" Wikipedia.com, accessed May 3, 2012,** http://en.wikipedia.org/wiki/Tax_rates_around_the_world.

The most globally competitive nations for corporations in 2008 were Singapore and Hong Kong.[12]

Placing federal extra taxes into reducing the total corporate (federal and state) tax level would position California's corporate tax rate below the most attractive nations to corporations—in the world.

_____

[12] **"Ease of doing business index" wikipedia.com, accessed May 3, 2012,**

http://en.wikipedia.org/wiki/Ease_of_Doing_Business_Index.

CALIFORNIA'S NEXT CENTURY 2.0

Trade calculations:

There is some evidence that about seven states might have a larger percentage of their economy related to foreign trade. However, this might not be so at all. There is a lot of evidence that services and technological trade, where ideas and products are shipped through the Internet (a major percentage of California exports and imports), may not be accurately tracked and "may be under-estimated by a considerable amount." Regardless, the combined money amount of all of these seven states is a fraction of the amount of money California alone makes.[13]

---

[13] Gus Koehler, *California Trade Policy* (California Research Bureau, 1999)

Citations for learning and verification:

Research and verify the main concepts, listed as titles only below, for yourself, at wikipedia.com. Other resources available online are posted just below the wiki search words.

Note: Possibly the oldest and most well-established scientific journal in the world, *Nature*, said that Wikipedia is as accurate as the *Encyclopedia Britannica*, possibly the oldest and most well-established reference series.[1] Furthermore, the

---

[1] Jim Giles, "Special Report: Internet Encyclopedias Go Head to Head," *Nature*, December 15, 2005, http://www.nature.com/nature/journal/v438/n7070/full/438900a.html.

oldest and most well-established university in America, Harvard, has multiple professors using Wikipedia as a source for their lectures.[2]

Although not the citation for this book, all of the concepts can be verified quickly with a review of these search words below—for each section—on Wikipedia.

CHAPTERS:

WHEN YOU LOOK AT A MAP OF THE NATIONS OF THE WORLD

Trade blocs, preferential trade areas, customs unions, free trade area, list of common

---

[2] Maxwell L. Child, "Professors Split on Wiki Debate," *The Harvard Crimson*, February 26, 2007, http://www.thecrimson.com/article/2007/2/26/professors-split-on-wiki-debate-despite/.

markets/single market, economic union, list of economic communities, FTAA, G8, G20, list of G20 summits, Doha development round, Shanghai Cooperation Organization, foreign policy of the United States, criticism of American foreign policy, IMF criticism, World Bank criticisms, UN, reform in the UN, US in UN, population density

AMERICA'S NEW MAP FOR THE NEXT CENTURY

Native Americans in the United States, Puerto Rico, Hawaii, California republic, American imperialism

THE NEW WAY TO "EMPIRE"

Commonwealth of Nations, Francophonia, Russians ethnic group outside of Russia, Overseas Chinese, Overseas Indians, Hungarian Diaspora, Swiss people, Turkish Diaspora, Filipino Diaspora, Jewish

Diaspora, cultural diplomacy, American Diaspora,

neocolonialism, Pan-Slavism, Pan-Turkism

Resources:
George T. Haley and Usha C. V. Haley, "Boxing with Shadows: Competing Effectively with the Overseas Chinese and Overseas Indian Business Networks in the Asian Arena," *Journal of Organizational Change Management*, Vol. 11 No. 4, (1998): 301-320

Gary G. Hamilton, *Stateless Economies: The Case of Overseas Chinese Capitalism (University of California, Davis: Department of Sociology, 1990)*

Evelyn Iritani, "Expatriates Play Key Role in Indians Economic Rise," *New York Times*, August 12, 2006.

Parag Khanna, "Waving Goodbye to Hegemony," *New York Times Magazine,* January 27, 2008.

Peter Leonard, "Russia's Putin Dreams of Sweeping Eurasian Union," *Associated Press* , January 3, 2012

Mandalit del Barco, "Filipino Biyam Balik: Gift Boxes Help Migrant Filipinos Keep Ties to Home," *NPR, May 4 2012*

Suhas L. Ketkar and Dilip Ratha. *Development Finance via Diaspora Bonds: Track Record and Potential,* (Washington D.C. : Migration and Development Conference at the World Bank, Held on May 23, 2007.)

"Israel-Diaspora Business Leadership Forum at Globes Business Conference," Jewish agency for Israel, accessed May 3 2012 http://www.jewishagency.org/JewishAgency/English /Israel/Partnerships/News/2007/news-0712-globes.htm

Vikas Maheshwari "Lessons for India from the Magic of Overseas Chinese!" Passionate about India (blog) September 9, 2011 http://arindamchaudhuri.blogspot.com/2011/09/le ssons-for-india-from-magic-of.html.

SUPERPOWERS OF THE FUTURE WORLD

BRIC, potential superpower, polarity in power

relations, power in international relations, foreign

relations People's Republic of China, foreign

relations of Russia, foreign relations of Brazil,

foreign relations of India, foreign relations of

CALIFORNIA'S NEXT CENTURY 2.0

Europe, foreign relations of America, polarity in international relations, Sino-Russian relations, Sino-American relations, Sino-Pacific relations, Sino-Indian relations, Brazil-America relations, the grand chessboard, the new great game, geo-strategy in central Asia .

References

THE OLD ORDER

Colonialism

Resources:
"2nd Industrial Revolution by Dragana Markovic"
Tesla 150th anniversary special, accessed May 3
2012,
http://www.b92.net/eng/special/tesla/life.php?nav_id=
36502

Joel Mokyr, 2nd Industrial Revolution,1870-1914,
(Evanston IL: Northwestern University, 1998)

Peter Cain, "British Free Trade 1850–1914,"
Refresh, Issue 29 (1999).

THE PREVIOUS ORDER

Soviet Empire, Cold War

THE WORLD NEEDS A NEW SWITZERLAND

FOR THE NEXT CENTURY

CALIFORNIA'S NEXT CENTURY 2.0

New world order, power in international relations, globalization, world economy, globality, Second Industrial Revolution, machine age

SWITZERLAND IS NOT DIVERSE FOR THIS WORLD "LIKE IT WAS"

Switzerland, Modern history of Switzerland, list of diplomatic missions in Switzerland, list of international organizations based in Geneva, Geneva, world economic forum,

Resources:
Christian H. Kalin, "Why Switzerland," *World wide banking, December 6, 2005,*

"Switzerland: The Colossal and Well Ordered Country," Thomas White, Global Investing, accessed May 3, 2012,
http://www.thomaswhite.com/explore-the-world/switzerland.aspx

CALIFORNIA'S NEXT CENTURY 2.0

Lauren Axelrod, "Switzerland: A Geographical and Economical Revolution of Travel and Responsibility,"*Trifter,* July 1, 2010 http://trifter.com/europe/switzerland-a-geographical-and-economical-revolution-of-travel-and-responsibility/

GLOBAL CONTENDERS FOR THE "NEW

SWITZERLAND FOR THE NEXT CENTURY"

Panama, Surinam, Israel, Hong Kong, Singapore,

California, Switzerland

WHY CALIFORNIA WOULD WANT THIS

Resource:
Andrew Chamberlain, "Why Do Some States Feast on Federal Spending, Not Others?" *Tax Foundation*, March 16, 2006, http://www.taxfoundation.org/blog/show/1397.html

EXAMPLES OF SUBNATIONAL

SOVEREIGNTY

CALIFORNIA'S NEXT CENTURY 2.0

Michael Keating, special administrative region, list of political parties campaigning for self-government, seceded, Catalan independentism, Scottish devolution, Alex Salmond, Greenland self-government referendum 2008, politics of Andorra, Liechtenstein government, San Marino, prefect, dominion, Egypt Roman province, republic-level commissariats for foreign affairs and defense of the USSR, Cyprus administrative divisions, Scottish government, Scotland within the UK, Scottish social attitudes survey, Scottish referendum bill 2010, special administrative region, commonwealth realms, dependent territory, associated state, dominion, Finland Cold War, history of Belarus, Ukraine Soviet Socialist Republic

Resources:

CALIFORNIA'S NEXT CENTURY 2.0

Phillip Bobbitt, *The Shield of Achilles: War, Peace, and the Course of History*, (New York: Knopf: 2002).[3]

Enrico Spolaore and Albert Alesina , *The Size of Nations*, (MIT Press: 2005).[4]

Michael Keating, *Nations Against the State: The New Politics of Nationalism in Quebec, Catalonia, and Scotland, (* Palgrave Macmillan*: 2002).*

Michael Keating, *Plurinational Democracy,* (Oxford University Press: 2005)

Joseph Y. S. Cheng, *Hong Kong Special Administrative Region, Looking After 10 Years* (City University of Hong Kong, 2007).

"Hong Kong Special Administrative Region" China.org, accessed May 3 2012 http://www.china.org.cn/english/feature/38096.htm

---

[3] Says that Quebec, Catalone, and Scotland innovations in government are the way the world is shifting (pgs. 801–2) and that Kurds, Quebec, and Catalonia are pursuing their own nations (pg. 782).

[4] Says that Quebec, Scotland, Catalone, and Basque have all pursued a strategy of decentralization that should be able to keep the federal system "healthy" (pg. 199).

CALIFORNIA'S NEXT CENTURY 2.0

Michael F. Martin, *Hong Kong 10 Years After Handover* (Washington DC: Congressional Research Service, 2007)

Anwen Elias "Whither a Europe of the Regions? Minority Nationalist Parties and the Challenges of European Integration," *Archive of European Integration*, (2007)

Simon Toubeau, *Social Democracy and Regional Nationalism in Multi-Level Systems* (University of Oxford: PSA Specialist Group Conference, British and Comparative Territorial Politics, 2010)

Michael Keating, "Stateless Nation-Building: Quebec, Catalonia and Scotland in the Changing State System," *Nations and Nationalism*, Volume 3, Issue 4, (2004)

"Adieu, Espana? The Road to Independence of Quebec, Scotland, Greenland and Catalonia," Catalonia Direct (blog). June 4, 2010, http://www.cataloniadirect.info/2010/06/adeu-espanya-independence-quebec-scotland-greenland-and-catalon/

Allen Buchanan, *Secession: The Morality of Political Divorce from Fort Sumter to Lithuania and Quebec*, (Westview press, 1999).

CALIFORNIA'S NEXT CENTURY 2.0

"On the record: Alex Salmond Interview," BBC1, accessed May 3 2012, http://www.bbc.co.uk/otr/intext95-96/Salmond10.3.96.html

APPENDIXES:

WHY CALIFORNIA AND AMERICA BOTH

WOULD ALLOW THIS

Optimum currency area, geographic determinism, social distance, other, alterity, secession, devolution, 2000s decade national sovereignty, currency union, red states and blue states, political ideologies in the United States, population density

DETAILS: RENAISSANCES ANALYSIS

Italian Renaissance, renaissance, Timbuktu, Kushan Empire, Bagram, Cahokia, Ptolemaic Dynasty,

CALIFORNIA'S NEXT CENTURY 2.0

Islamic golden age, Alhambra, London, Silk Road, Carolingian Dynasty, Tibet, Dejima

DETAILS: COMPETITIVE ADVANTAGE OF BEING THE NEW SWITZERLAND FOR THE NEXT CENTURY

International trade, absolute advantage, Ricardian economics, comparative advantage, new trade theory, national diamond, diamond model, Michael Porter, Porter 5 forces analysis, techno cluster, economies of agglomeration, factors proportions models: Heckscher-Ohlin, product life cycle, country size theory or new trade theory by Paul Krugman

Resources:

CALIFORNIA'S NEXT CENTURY 2.0

Michael Porter, *Competitive Advantage of Nations* (New York: The Free Press, 1990)

"What is New Trade Theory?" <u>Alex Tabarrok</u>, accessed May 3 2012, <u>http://marginalrevolution.com/marginalrevolution/200 8/10/what-is-new-tra.html</u>

"International Trade Theory," UWF.edu, accessed May 3 2012, http://www.uwf.edu/rsjoland/WEB%20POSTED %20FILES/6%20International%20Trade%20The ory%20A%202%2004.pdf

NOTES

NOTES

NOTES

NOTES

NOTES

NOTES

CALIFORNIA'S NEXT CENTURY 2.0

NOTES

NOTES

Mikazuki Publishing House Titles

Mikazuki Jujitsu Manual

25 Principles of Martial Arts

Karate 360

Political Advertising Manual

Learning Magic

Stories of a Street Performer; Memoirs of a Master Magician

Magic as Science & Religion

The Bribe Vibe

Small Arms & Deep Pockets

Arctic Black Gold

Find the Ideal Husband

John Locke's 2nd Treatise on Civil Government

The History of Acid Tripping

I Dream In Haiku

Mikazuki Political Science Manual

Tokiwa; A Japanese Love Story

The Card Party; Theater Play

Hagakure; The Book of Hidden Leaves

MMA Coloring Book

DIY Comic Book

Freakshow Los Angeles

Swords & Sails: The Legacy of the Red Lion

Palloncino

**MIKAZUKI PUBLISHING HOUSE
BELIEVES THAT EDUCATION IS
THE KEY TO HAPPINESS**

www.MikazukiPublishingHouse.com